MW01595248

We Walk By Faith, Not By Sight: Women of Faith in the Marketplace Vol. 2

Compiled by Kristi Lynn Olson

Co-authored by:

Lemmonstine Poindexter

Danielle Lee

Gale Gillespie

Patti Ann Ridgway

Victoria Soto, JD

Lori Reese Patton

Bren Olsen

Danita Scott

Betsy Lavin

We Walk By Faith, Not By Sight: Women of Faith in the
Marketplace Vol.2

We Walk By Faith, Not By Sight: Women of Faith in the
Marketplace Vol.2

Religion / Christian Life / Professional Growth

ISBN-10: 1544113307
ISBN-13: 978-1544113302
Religion / Christian Life / Professional Growth

Table of Contents

Walking by faith is a journey, and for Christian women who work in the marketplace that journey can be particularly challenging as they strive to do their job with excellence AND be salt and light to a world filled with challenges.

To have faith means to always have a vision of what success looks like for YOU, and to stay encouraged and engaged in your faith as you walk that out daily. And sometimes everything around you looks like an insurmountable obstacle. That's when you need faith like never before. That's when you must be confident in what you see in your spirit and not be swayed by what you see with your eyes in the natural. The apostle Paul knew this struggle all too well and wrote, "for we walk by faith, not by sight [living our lives in a manner consistent with our confident belief in God's promises]"— 2 Corinthians 5:7 AMP

The women who bravely share their stories here on the following pages have influenced those around them in a variety of industries, yet they all have one thing in common. They have learned to navigate their role in the marketplace as they live consistent and confident in God's promises for their lives. May their stories inspire, equip, and encourage you to keep pressing on as you walk by faith and not by sight!

Love and Blessings,
Kristi Lynn Olson
Founder & CEO, Women Infused™

LEMMONSTINE POINDEXTER

Tell us about who you are, your profession, and how you use the unique gifts God gave you to impact your circle of influence for His Purposes in the workplace.

My name is Lemmonstine Poindexter. I am the 7th of 9 children (8 of which are girls). My father was 70 years old when I was born, and he passed away in 2000 at the age of 104. These facts are important because they play an important part in who I am, and how my upbringing set the path for my life. Because my parents were older (my father much older than my mom), we were always around older people. My parents taught us the importance of God, education, and respect of others. These three things have shaped my life.

I am a supervisor in the customer relations section for a large public utility company. I have been with my current employer for 30 years this year. I started with this company when I was 20 years old. I have held my current title as supervisor for the last 16 years. Before holding that title, I was a trainer for our section (Customer Relations) for a few years.

I feel that God has strategically placed me in my position so that I can provide a word of encouragement for customers and employees. Daily, I encounter many customers who need assistance with their utility bills. Although I am required to make decisions based upon policies and procedures already established by my company, I am constantly faced with the need to show empathy and compassion. The people that I speak with on most days are facing financial struggles. I always pray that God will allow me to look past their current situation, and my own thoughts, so that I will be able to discern those who are truly in need of assistance. I grew up with very little financially, but more than most when it came to loving parents, morals, and Christianity. I try to never forget where I came from.

I believe one of the greatest gifts God has given me is the gift of encouragement…whether through the written word, singing, or spoken word. As a supervisor for the last 16 years, I have learned the importance of listening; listening past the things that are said. I have found in the workplace that many of the stressors that employees face is not actually brought about by the workplace, but are issues that started in their homes. We all face stress in life, and when we must come to work and still perform to a certain level of productivity, this increases the stress.

I have endured stress in my own life during the last 30 years of my employment. I have dealt with divorce, struggled with the realities of my own infertility, and many other things. Yet, I believe these things have helped me, as a supervisor, to understand the importance of allowing God to flow through me to help others. With the help of God, I have been able to come to work with a smile on my face and remain productive. Due to the issues that I have faced, I have learned how to positively influence the lives of those around me. I have learned the importance of empathy!

Many times, employees and coworkers simply need to be heard, or need a word of encouragement. I have found that there is usually a root cause when employees are not productive. They are usually going through some sort of crisis or ongoing situation in their personal lives. I am thankful that our company offers an Employee Assistance Program (EAP). There have been many times that I have referred employees to this program, as it is a very confidential program.

As a Christian woman, I realize that we should take our burdens to the Lord. However, in the workplace, there is a fine line between giving people godly advice and professional advice. I often pray that people will see the God that lives in me, and will want that for themselves. God is the only one who has given me the peace that I have. Obtaining my Master's Degree in Counseling has also provided me with tools needed in the workplace, because, as a supervisor, I have had to assume many roles. One of those roles seems to be the role of a counselor. Yet, I also believe that referring them to the EAP will allow them to make the first step in resolving their personal issues.

You are called to be 'the salt and light' in this world. How do you see yourself fulfilling that command by working in the marketplace?

Matthew 5:13-16 (The Message Bible) puts it this way when describing the salt and light:

[13] *"Let me tell you why you are here. You're here to be salt-seasoning that brings out the God-flavors of this earth. If you lose your saltiness, how will people taste godliness? You've lost your usefulness and will end up in the garbage.* [14-16] "Here's another way to put it: You're here to be light, bringing out the God-colors in the world. God is not a secret to be kept. We're going public with this, as public as a city on a hill. If I make you light-bearers, you don't think I'm going to hide you under a bucket, do you? I'm putting you on a light stand. Now that I've put you there on a hilltop, on a light stand—shine! Keep open house; be generous with your lives. By opening up to others, you'll prompt people to open up with God, this generous Father in heaven."

By working in the marketplace, I believe that I am on display, and consider it an honor to show the love of God. I am there to lift the lowly spirit, to share a smile, to give an encouraging word. I am there to motivate, to give constructive feedback, to share wisdom and advice. Everything that I do (or don't do) or say represents my Christianity. It does not fulfill the commands of Matthew 5:13-16 if I am only in the presence of other believers or those who call themselves Christians. A light that is shining among light is barely seen. However, a light shining in darkness is easily recognizable. Being in the marketplace allows me to go public with the characteristics of Christ. Although it is a common statement, it is true. *"People care more about what you do than what you say."*

It is my prayer that my light is continually shining so that others may desire to know where my joy and peace comes from. It can be uncomfortable to be constantly on display, but I have learned that people do not expect you to be perfect. They just want you to real, and to be who you say you are. In the workplace, I strive every day to treat others as I wish to be treated. This does not mean that I always hit the mark, but it is my goal.

How do you structure your time to reflect all the priorities and opportunities God has given you to be a light for him without losing yourself in the process, both personally and professionally?

I spend more time in the workplace than I do at home, with family, or friends. It is difficult to structure time around all the opportunities that God has given me. After spending 8 (actually 9) hours a day in the workplace, and over 40 hours a week, my mind, body, and spirit can surely feel exhausted. However, I ask God for strength. It is important for me to have time to focus on my writing and music. I am learning to not take on more than I can possibly do. I have learned to say no to some engagements, whether they are professional, personal, or spiritual in nature. I try to make the best use of my work day, so that I do not have to put in extra hours to complete my tasks.

When asked if I can attend an event, I do not give a quick answer. I check my calendar, look at my week or month and then get back with the person who has invited me. It is important to keep your focus on the purpose that you know God has given you. Many times, we can be as busy as a bee; yet busy doing the wrong things. We can become busy doing things that God has not even called us to do. I have learned to remove myself from things that take up a great deal of my time, that do not move me in the direction of my life purpose(s). There are times that we must face the reality of things.

As a single woman, I know that my career is very important, as it provides the finances for the things that I desire to do. I am very realistic about my need to have a steady income. Thus, I realize that everything else in my life must be worked around that time. Since I work for a large public utility, at times I am called in to work during weather-related storms, etc. I know that this is a part of my job, so I remain aware of this when accepting any types of ministry engagements. I always make sure that I take the proper steps to take time off from work if I have agreed to some sort of engagement.

Sundays are my day of worship, rest and time with family for dinner, so I do not book anything. Sunday night is my time to refocus my mind for the workweek ahead. I schedule vacation time for the year at the beginning of each year, and try to schedule something for each quarter. Vacation time can be anything from a few hours on a Friday, to a weekend, to a week off in the summer and year end. These things are important to me, and I encourage all women to do this, so that they can keep their sanity. This allows you to not lose yourself in the process of everything else you have going on in life.

As a woman of faith, how do you integrate biblical and spiritual principles into your work environment with grace and truth?

I love the way that the Message Bible makes the Word of God understandable. It is like reading a book. I have tried to use the simplicity of the Message Bible as an example of how I integrate biblical and spiritual principles into my work environment. It is very possible to speak truths to people without having to quote scripture. I try to use life stories the way that Jesus used the parables. Also, every individual is different and we must remain aware of that as we communicate to others in the work place. What works for one person, will not work for another. People have different upbringings, lifestyles, and beliefs. I believe in treating others as we want to be treated, we share our biblical and spiritual principles with grace and truth. If someone asks about my faith and what I believe, I do not hesitate to share with them. I try to think before I speak. The scriptures remind us that *"A fool uttereth all his mind: but a wise man keepeth it in till afterwards." Proverbs 29:11*

Everyone needs a "Sabbath Rest". Even God rested after the six days of creation. How do you create space to recharge, refresh, and refocus?

My "Sabbath Rest" is on Saturdays. There are many Saturdays that I have different things going on, but it is the exception, and not the norm. It also depends on the time of year. I always look at my month of Saturdays. I try to make sure I have at least one Saturday each month that I can spend at home. There are only a few months each year that this does not happen for me. *I want to note here that this has not always been the case.* For over 20 years, my Saturdays were filled with ministry or church events, church meetings, door-to-door evangelism, etc. As I have grown older, and wiser, I have learned that for me, that is not a good way to live. It only burns you out, and causes you to want to hide away whenever you can get a moment. That does not allow you to shine at all, if you are always tired.

I enjoy Saturdays and Sunday evenings in my home, especially when there is no TV on. Just peace and quiet. I find that I need darkness and quiet to truly get into my "secret" space. This space allows me to recharge, refresh, and refocus. I come from a large family, so when we are together there is lot of noises and chatter, but fun. However, when I am home, I truly enjoy the peace and quiet. Don't get me wrong, I enjoy a Saturday when I can get up, open my curtains, let the sun shine in, get back in bed, and watch movies or Food Network all day.

Being a night owl, I also enjoy the quietness that comes after midnight, and just lying in bed thinking about life. A great deal of my time to refocus comes in the middle of the night. I believe this is when God speaks to me the most. It may just be that this is the time I am the most still and quiet, and able to hear what He has been trying to speak to me all day. I believe that this season of my life is just the beginning of God using me for His true purpose that He has laid out for me. I have had to learn many lessons from all the other seasons to prepare me for this one.

As a woman of faith, what has been your biggest obstacle or challenge in the workplace, and how did you navigate that successfully?

As a woman of faith, one of my biggest challenges has been trying to help employees or customers with their issues without telling them that I believe their real issue is that they need a true relationship with God and faith that He will do what He said He will do. We all face similar issues at some point in our lives. So, I just try to show them the love of Christ, and give them real life examples from my own life of what God has done for me. I help them to see the importance of making the best of each day and the need to make the best decisions for their life. I try to point them in the right direction, to find the proper resources.

Have you ever felt 'guilty' for having a career or working? How did you resolve that, and where do you find mentors or support for your journey?

No, I have never felt guilty for having a career or working. I have never believed that God's plan for me life was to hide me under a bushel (although I have often thought it would be nice for a moment).

How did you choose your career, or did it choose you?

I believe it was half and half. I always thought I would work in business, in an office. But I did not plan where I would do this, and had no idea when I took a part time summer job, I would still be there 30 years later. In high school, my focus was in business education at our vocational school. When I was a sophomore in college, I participated in a summer work program. We were placed at different agencies and companies during the summer. I worked as a junior clerk for my current employer, a public utility. I was only to work there from June through August, until school started again. I worked in a section of the company that helped senior citizens and the disabled obtain assistance to pay their utility bills. Before my summer internship ended, a job posting became available in that same section. I applied and was offered the job. I never planned to stay there. I was simply going to work at this company until I graduated from college. (I am so thankful that God keeps us despite the foolishness of our youthful thinking. My 20-year-old self, did not realize that I was at a company with great benefits.)

I went from that job (as a junior clerk) to becoming a customer service advisor, then a trainer, and finally to the position I hold now as a supervisor. Since I was working full time, I had to begin going to school at night to complete my undergraduate degree in Business Administration. A few years later, I enrolled in school again and completed my Masters of Art in Counseling. I pursued the master's degree as a personal goal for myself, as I knew I would need this for the remainder of my life. I am also a Certified Life Coach, and work with our Counseling Ministry at church. I believe God will continue to use the leadership skills I have gained in the workplace, and education I have obtained, to do His will even when my employment has ended. God has always put me in an arena to influence the lives of others.

If you could give your 'younger self' any advice on integrating your faith life and your work life, what would it be? Would you do anything differently?

I would remind myself that it is okay to be human and to acknowledge the hurts, pains, and disappointments of life. I would remind myself that it is okay to stand up for yourself, while still maintaining your integrity and faith. I don't know if there is much that I would do differently though. I have tried to maintain my character in the face of adversity during my work life.

How has your work challenged your faith, character, or values, and how have you been able to resolve that without compromising?

I believe that my work has always challenged my faith and values, but in a positive way. It has challenged me to speak the right things, and do the right things. It has challenged me to find ways to share my faith in the workplace without being overbearing or judgmental. It has challenged me to uphold the ethical standards of my company while also balancing their standards with my own. I don't really my feel my work has caused me to compromise my values or standards at all.

Some women feel 'less spiritual' when working in a full-time career. How do you develop your spiritual life amid a demanding work life?

I have not felt less spiritual at all. I feel I have had to remain spiritual to make it in the workplace. Developing a spiritual life during a demanding work life begins at home. I must set aside time for daily prayer and devotions before the day begins, or at the end of the day. I am not always successful, but I continue to strive for it. However, I pray throughout each day that God would be with me, and would give me wisdom and strength. If there is a pressing issue, whether personal or professional, I can always pray a quiet prayer, or find a place to pray. I keep a song in my heart all the time.

As a supervisor, there have been many times that I had to initiate uncomfortable meetings, reviews, and performance appraisals. I have learned to pray before any of these uncomfortable scheduled meetings, so that God will help me to say the right things and to present the information in the best way that I can. In situations that are unplanned and situations that are very confrontational, I pray that God gives me the strength to keep my own attitude in check. I pray each day for a level head, and a good attitude. God is always with me, so it does not matter where I am. His spirit lives in me.

What is your favorite scripture, and how has that influenced your role as a woman who works and walks by faith?

My favorite scripture is *Isaiah 54:1*. *"Sing, O barren, thou that didst not bear; break forth into singing, and cry aloud, thou that didst not travail with child: for more are the children of the desolate than the children of the married wife, saith the LORD. "* KJV

I love *Isaiah 54:1-6 The Message Bible reads: [Spread Out! Think Big!] "Sing,* **barren woman**, *who has never had a baby. Fill the air with song, you who've never experienced childbirth! You're ending up with far more children than all those childbearing women." God says so! "Clear lots of ground for your tents! Make your tents large. Spread out! Think big! Use plenty of rope, drive the tent pegs deep. You're going to need lots of elbow room for your growing family. You're going to take over whole nations; you're going to resettle abandoned cities. Don't be afraid, you're not going to be embarrassed. Don't hold back, you're not going to come up short. You'll forget all about the humiliations of your youth, and the indignities of being a widow will fade from memory. For your Maker is your bridegroom, his name, God-of-the-Angel-Armies! Your Redeemer is The Holy of Israel, known as God of the whole earth. You were like an abandoned wife, devastated with grief, and God welcomed you back, Like a* **woman** *married young and then left, " says your God.*

It was during the most difficult time of my life that this scripture came to me. I was going through a terrible divorce and coming to terms with the fact that I would probably never bear a child. I was also in the midst of leaving a church (and city) that I had served faithfully in for over 20 years. I was leaving all the friends that I had spent many years serving with. I was also trying to begin my writing and music career. Then God sent me this scripture. It spoke more to me than anything I had ever heard. This scripture became the title of my first published book "Sing O Barren Woman". I see God bringing those words of Isaiah 54:1-6 to pass in my life with each day that I live! I have learned to "Dance in the Rain."

Learn more about Lemmonstine Poindexter

Lemmonstine Poindexter ("Lemon") is the founder of National Barren Women's Support Groups, a group designed to encourage barren women. She is the author of "Sing O' Barren Woman", and has released two cd's: "Dancing In the Rain" in 2012 and "More Than I Deserve" in 2016.

Her love for writing and singing will continue to serve as an outlet to minister to others. Lemon received her Masters of Art in Counseling from Liberty University in 2014. She plans to open a life-coaching center for women. Above all else, she loves God and wants to serve Him by serving others. Her challenge to women: "Dance and Sing!" (even in the rain).

For more information, visit her webpage at
www.lemmonstinepoindexter.org

DANIELLE LEE

Tell us about who you are, your profession, and how you use the unique gifts God gave you to impact your circle of influence for His Purposes in the workplace.

I am the daughter of the King, follower of Christ, wife of almost fourteen years to the love of my life Stephen, proud mother to Elijah (6), Gabriel (5), Joshua (4), and Isabella (3), Executive Consultant with Ambit Energy, and the owner of a microblading (semi-permanent eyebrow tattooing) salon called Brow Elegance.

As an Executive Consultant with Ambit Energy I train other consultants on the art of gathering customers, showing them how to build a strong organization, and create loyal relationships with new business partners and customers. There are times when we travel outside of our home to go to business meetings or training sessions, but much of my time working is spent with my husband/business partner in our home office. I must stay very focused on our goals and stay self-motivated while working from home. To engage my creative side, I started an eyebrow tattooing salon. I love seeing people's confidence change just by helping them love their brows.

One unique gift God gave me is I am great encourager. I have a gift of making any individual feel like they are the most important person in the world when talking to them. Being able to learn about another person makes my day. I really do love people and care about them. I have no problem going up to a stranger and starting a conversation with them. That is something that blesses me. That is why I firmly believe the network marketing business is a great fit for my personality. Because I constantly love change I feel like the brow business is perfect for me too.

You are called to be 'the salt and light' in this world. How do you see yourself fulfilling that command by working in the marketplace?

By continually working on my relationship with the Lord to hear him clearly and being obedient to whatever he asks of me. Having a sensitivity to other people's needs. When we were struggling financially, we could focus only on our own family's concerns. Now, I feel like we have more of a sensitivity to help others who need prayers or have a financial need.

I really believe I was called to be a light in the marketplace. In the marketplace, it is such a great place to show the love of Christ. There are people from all walks of life coming together with a common goal for success and belonging. I love being able to share about Jesus. I know God has given me the gift of empathy. There have been several situations where I have had many people tell me how I have lifted their spirits with words that blessed them when they were feeling so low. I make a great cheerleader. In my position, I am constantly cheering people up, helping people not be hard on themselves, and loving people.

How do you structure your time to reflect all the priorities and opportunities God has given you to be a light for him without losing yourself in the process, both personally and professionally?

I use this as a model, God first, family second, and work is third. Keeping God in first place is most important because I can't be all that I can be without him filling me up with his word, his love, and encouragement. I always know my day will be off centered when I don't spend time with him in worship and in prayer. That is why I like to focus the early morning spending time with God in his word before the kids all wake up. My husband and I love praying for our kids before they leave the house for school. We always pray they are bright shining light and represent Jesus everywhere they go. I love attending marriage conferences with my husband at church because we want our kids to feel secure in their home that mommy and daddy love each other very much. I also enjoy taking a class at church with my husband that has a subject that will help our family walk closer to Jesus, and we attending church weekly is a huge priority. Church is my life source a blessing for my family.

My husband and I lost both of our moms in 2015. It was one of the hardest years of my life and my husband's life. We both were very close to our moms. When they passed away it was a very busy time in our lives. Life is already crazy when you have four young children so after our moms died we both hid our pain by keeping ourselves incredibly busy. We put all their pictures away because it was too hard to look at them without wanting to cry our eyes out. So, when our church told us recently they were offering a grief support class at church I knew we needed to prioritize doing that.

It is never easy to face pain head on but we both knew it was important to make this class a priority every week. One of our biggest goals when we partnered working with Ambit Energy was to be able to have freedom and flexibility in our work schedule that didn't interfere with our family priorities. There is a lot of wiggle room in our schedule. We make time for things that edify God and family. We also make time for things that help us build all our businesses like classes, trainings, meeting with mentors, going to conferences and important events to continue learning. Also, I trained with the top company in the world that specializes in microblading so I am constantly working on my skills.

As a woman of faith, how do you integrate biblical and spiritual principles into your work environment with grace and truth?

"Whatever you do, work at it with all your heart, as working for the Lord, not for human masters" - Colossians 3:23

Work as though I am working unto the Lord. I am reminded all the time that he sees everything. I am accountable to him for the way I act. I know that he watches how I conduct myself in all my interactions on the phone and in person. I fall short many times but I know God is full of grace and mercy to help me. He also wants me to do things with excellence.

Everyone needs a "Sabbath Rest". Even God rested after the six days of creation. How do you create space to recharge, refresh, and refocus?

I don't like to work on Sundays so I try to make it a priority to keep that day for rest, refocus and recharge. I attend a wonderful church with my family. We have made it a tradition to have a nice meal together after we attend, and spend the rest of the day as a family. I try to avoid taking any business calls on Sundays. One thing my husband and I also learned was keeping the kids in two services so we can attend the first service together and then during the second service we will either volunteer together or just grab a coffee in the church lounge and go over what our week is looking like. It always helps us to have good communication to find out where we need to focus and set goals for the week in our family and in our business. I come into the Lord's presence in worship at church, humbling myself by going down to the altar and asking for prayer when I need it which is all the time. I get things off my chest so I don't hold onto the weight of worries and troubles. Coming into agreement with other believers. It is not healthy to hold on to our worries alone. I am thankful to have an extremely supportive husband who allows me to step out of the house for a few hours to get my nails done or go grocery shopping alone. By giving me this alone time it helps me refocus and reenergizes me for the work week. My husband is also an extremely talented hairstylist and when all the kids go to bed he will color my grey hair and give me a nice haircut. Those things make a huge difference in my confidence.

As a woman of faith, what has been your biggest obstacle or challenge in the workplace, and how did you navigate that successfully?

Time management is one of my biggest challenges. There is so much I want to do and accomplish. It is challenging balancing the time between two businesses that I love while still working on being a great wife to my husband, mother to my children, and friend to the people I love. I also struggle saying "no" to people, being an approval addict or people pleaser, and wanting everyone to be happy. I have learned that it is perfectly fine to ask for help or tell someone "no". I want to be an example of Christ everywhere I go. I struggle speaking up for myself and asking for help so now I am slowly learning its ok to ask for help. It doesn't mean I am inadequate it just means I am human and need help from time to time and to just receive.

Have you ever felt 'guilty' for having a career or working? How did you resolve that, and where do you find mentors or support for your journey?

Yes, I have struggled and felt 'guilty' for having a career. My mom was a stay at home mother and so was my mother-in-law. Every woman is equipped differently though and I always loved the opportunity to work and help contribute financially to our family. I have felt bad for closing the office door or staying in the car much longer than expected to complete a business task. I hate missing out on things but I am so thankful for the provision God has blessed our family with through the electricity business. I always dreamed of having a family vacation with the kids and we put it on our dream board. Last summer we were able to take the kids to the Alabama Coast and witness seeing them touch the ocean for the first time and walk on white sand beaches. I constantly remind myself when I am working late at the salon or just in the home office, this is why. So, we can make wonderful memories as a family and see our children's faces light up spending quality time with them. My children are all still young and there are four of them and I want to value every precious moment I can.

My husband and I make it a priority to go on dates with our kids alone at least once a week or once every two weeks. It is a recharge for me and my husband to enjoy the time with them one on one and connect with them. It is funny how different children act alone versus being with their siblings. That alone time helps me to not feel guilty when I am working.

I do believe some of the best mentors are the ones at church or small groups who are also in the marketplace and in a different season of life with their kids (maybe they are older). I have a mentor mom in one of my groups who prays for me, calls me and encourages me during this very busy season of life being a mom to young ones and balancing business and careers.

How did you choose your career, or did it choose you?

I believe my career chose me. I never in my life thought I would be selling & marketing electricity, or tattooing! I have watched and seen others succeed in these same professions and thought "I can do that!" I have always gravitated to positions that were working with people. I really have seen the hand of God on me and how he has orchestrated my professional life even before I became a Christian.

There was a time in my early twenties when I wanted to get a flight attendant position. I just knew that I knew I was supposed to be a flight attendant. I interviewed with a company I really wanted to get hired with. I got to the third interview where they flew me to Chicago and then they declined me for the position. I was so discouraged when I got the "no" for the position. However, I had an interview with another airline who offered me a flight attendant position. I gladly accepted the position. I loved flying, it was so fun to see places I had never seen before and meet new people all the time.

After living in the world and out of my suitcase, I still felt like something was missing. I went on a trip shortly after 9/11 and another flight attendant witnessed to me and shared with me about Christ. He asked me if I died today would I be sure I was going to heaven or hell? I thought I would be going to heaven, he asked why, and I said I was a good person. He said, can I show you some things? He brought out his bible and shared with me several scriptures that brought conviction to my heart and it gave me a great revelation that I was living wrong and selfishly. So, while we were sitting on an empty plane in first class, I gave my life to Christ. We were delayed five hours after getting a flat tire in Chicago.

Each time I am delayed at the airport the thought always crosses my mind, is a person being shared the good news about Christ? I call it a divine delay. I am so thankful to God that even though I got a "no" from something I thought I wanted that God was setting me up for something even greater. His thoughts and plans are greater than our plans. Not only did my life change after I came home from that trip but that other flight attendant gave me a bible and some additional resources like books and CD's as I started my walk as a Christian. It is such a small world but one of those books that he gave me was written by Ed Decker. Ed was the one who ended up marrying my husband and I. Our only pre-marriage counseling session happened at Ed's house a month prior to our wedding day and this was the first time I met him. As my husband and I sat in his office prior to speaking to him I started noticing in his library books he had written. And then it all clicked, this was all a God ordained moment and all the dots were connected. He was a pastor at the church we attended in Seattle and his children and wife both were clients of my husbands. God is so amazing.

If you could give your 'younger self' any advice on integrating your faith life and your work life, what would it be? Would you do anything differently?

I would tell my younger self to value time and relationships. Life is too short. After losing family members at young ages I value the time with people in my life. We never know when God is going to call us home. Things we think are such a big deal aren't really. I would say not have stupid fights with family or people at work. We think we always must be right and that is not true.

Never live in regret, love fully and forgive quickly. Don't hold on to grudges. Always believe the best about people, and pray for your enemies. Supernatural blessings come when you forgive. Pray for people the way the Lord would see them and pray for our enemies. Accept yourself as God made you. I spent too many years fighting this battle and it took a long time to surrender, and by that time it carried extremely painful ramifications. How I wish I could tell the young me that it is okay to be true to yourself. God does not make mistakes. Listen to the Holy Spirit for guidance.

How has your work challenged your faith, character, or values, and how have you been able to resolve that without compromising?

We moved to Texas in 2011 to pursue our electricity business. We were in prayer and counsel for many years before we made the move. When we finally felt like God was opening the door for us to move to Texas from Washington State we walked into one of the most trying times of our lives. We arrived in Texas and literally all hell broke loose and things did not work out the way we expected when we moved here. We had a disagreement with the only family we knew in Texas who was in the same business and we had a falling out in our relationship and we were left bitter, hopeless, and discouraged.

We were so down for the first three and a half years in Texas. A lot of our discouragement came from regret that we weren't doing what we believed God called us here to do and what we told all of our family and friends we would do. We struggled financially for so long and we were used to feeling defeated. My husband is a talented hairstylist and when we moved to Texas he had to start over building a clientele. That was not an easy task. Life got so hard that we thought it was time to throw in the towel and move back to Seattle. We thought maybe we missed God's plan moving to Texas.

We called all our family and friends and said we are moving back to Seattle. The very next morning we both had a strong conviction and we both heard the Holy Spirit say "I didn't tell you it was ok to leave, I brought you here." We called our families and said, "no, it's not happening". So many people told us we missed God moving to Texas. We even had family tell us they would pay for everything just to move us back to Seattle. We stayed true to what God said and we stayed and stood on the word he gave us to be in Texas. We could've easily taken the financial help and moved back. It was not easy to say no to the financial help to move back but during this time the Lord taught us a huge lesson that he is our provider for everything and he will never let us down and he always took care of us in so many miraculous ways. We always had a roof over our heads, food on the table and gas in our gas tank. We remember going to church the last day of the month many times and not having rent money for the next day. We went down for prayer and miraculously our rent was paid within the following day or week. Our families, friends, our church, and charities stood by us through prayer and everything.

In May of 2015, only one month after we started seeing a breakthrough in our business we went to Seattle to be with my husband's mom during the last month of her life. Because our business was so flexible and we weren't tied down to a job we picked up and flew our family to Seattle to be with my husband's family. It wasn't easy seeing my mother in-law in her state. She just had a surgery to remove a brain tumor and her gorgeous hair was shaved off. She barely spoke and the cancer had aged her quickly. I always was so thankful how she and my father in-law stood by us during past hard financial times.

In fact, if it was the year prior there was no way we could've flown our whole family out to be with her and spend so much time with her before she died. I am so thankful to God that our business was taking off and we could cover our bills in Texas so we could fully focus on being there with my mother in law. We had four young children with us, big goals with our company and extreme sadness going to hospice every day with the little ones. My husband and I made a decision that we would work hard in the morning and early afternoon then after 2pm we made the forty-five minute drive to the hospice care facility to spend the rest of the day with my husband's mom. We would stay sometimes up till 10pm at night with four little ones and then start over and do the same thing the next day. It was a rewarding time as we were reaching huge goals we dreamed about hitting after partnering with our company but we also dealt with some of the greatest losses we could encounter.

I was very close with my mother. She didn't live close but I was always just a phone call away from her. During the time, we lost my husband's mom we went to Oregon to see my mom a couple times. I will never forget the last night I saw her before we flew back to Texas. We spent a good part of the day visiting and she always gave me great advice about raising kids. She loved Jesus. My husband had the privilege ten years ago, leading my mom to Christ. I am forever thankful he did. Because of his obedience, I know I will see her again in heaven. Our business was challenged during these incredibly hard times losing our precious moms. We made a choice to persevere and overcome. It was only God that we walked through this with grace. So many people give up during challenging times but we know we needed to both stay strong for our family and keep trusting God's promises.

With God's favor, we got to the second highest position in the company in less than six months (normally it can take an average person three to five years working hard), we earned a five-star trip to Hawaii with the owners of our company and top leaders and we were the top 50 income earners in our company last year. We really believe that God blessed us because of the fact that we never gave up despite how hard things got. We also believe because we finally forgave each other and stopped blaming each other for our past hurts and mistakes, and we also forgave everyone in our lives that ever hurt us. We allowed forgiveness to fill our hearts and God supernaturally blessed our businesses.

Some women feel 'less spiritual' when working in a full-time career. How do you develop your spiritual life amid a demanding work life?

I feel it is so important to keep the word of God right on my desk. I can go to it when I need help, guidance or just encouragement when things are not going well that day. We always pray for our kids right before they leave for school and it blesses and encourages us to set the stage for the day. I keep these faith cards on my desk that have a scripture on it and a key word on it. I look to those cards to help me get through the day. Here is an example of one: it reads in big letters GENEROSITY - giving what we have so others feel God's love. There is also a scripture on it: this one reads Command them to do good, to be rich in good deeds, and to be generous and willing to share- 1 Timothy 6:18.

Sometimes I will also get on my Pandora app on my phone and just tune out phone calls and listen to a few worship songs to get focused. I make time for things that will help me grow as a believer in Christ. I always make it a priority to be at church, volunteer, and get involved in groups at church for fellowship and to build relationships with other believers (you are who you hang out with). I participate in groups and classes with my husband to grow as followers of Christ. It is so important to be in a church that will help you grow in your faith. I pray for the Lord to work through my hands to create his best results. Pray for the success of people on our team. I expect God to do miracles in my life.

What is your favorite scripture, and how has that influenced your role as a woman who works and walks by faith?

Jeremiah 29:11 – "For I know the plans that I have for you, says the Lord, plans for peace and not for evil, to give you a future and a hope". This has influenced me to know that God is a good father and wants only the best for me and my future. When things get hard and when things are good I go to this scripture for encouragement to keep pressing forward. Before we had children, we were asked to consider being foster parents to my cousin's two-month old baby. She was going through a hard time and got in trouble with the law. They took the baby away from her, and the state was trying to place the baby with a family member. They looked at placing the baby with us or the father's cousin. We started walking through the steps to become foster parents. We had been married six years and didn't have any children yet but we started imagining having a baby in our house.

I always knew I wanted to be a mom (I was always babysitting as a young girl and I also had three little brothers), so we started getting really excited at the thought of a new baby girl coming to our house. Well, the doors closed and they rejected us. The baby was in Oregon and we were in Washington and they wanted to keep the baby in the same state as the baby's parents. We were devastated but accepted the outcome. During the process when they were deciding on us or the other family we went to a group at our church where they wanted to pray for us.

During the group meeting one of the women who was there had her newborn son with her and felt like God was telling her to place the baby in my husband's arms. As my husband held the baby something broke in the spirit and brought healing to his heart about being a dad. When my husband was twelve years old his youngest brother passed away. His brother was only six months old. It was a very tough time for him and his family and for many years he struggled with the thought of being a parent due to this incredible loss he had when he was a young boy.

In some ways, we both were scared about being parents, but he especially did not want to lose another baby or fall in love with another baby only to have it taken away. We both knew God was calling us to walk through the foster to adopt process. As we walked through those doors he brought healing from past wounds. That scripture was saying that I know the plans I have for you are for peace and not evil. Well, when the door closed less than a month later we found out we were pregnant with our first-born son Elijah!

We were so excited and felt like God was rewarding us for being faithful and obeying him walking through what we walked through. God doesn't forget details and cares about us and wants us to be healed. He knows the hurts and fears and wounds that we carry, and wants to deliver us from that bondage and bless us.

Learn more about Danielle Lee

 Danielle Lee has parlayed her communication skills and natural talent for networking into successful stints as a flight attendant, insurance agent and an investment advisor helping parents make college a reality for their children. With a growing family to take care of, Danielle and her husband Stephen became consultants for Ambit Energy, a company that allowed them the flexibility to work from home. She and her husband rose to the rank of Executive Consultant, and in 2016 became one of Ambit's top 50 income-earning consultants. Danielle resides in Fort Worth, Texas, with her husband and their four young children.

GALE GILLESPIE

Tell us about who you are, your profession, and how you use the unique gifts God gave you to impact your circle of influence for His Purposes in the workplace.

I am a black woman of faith. The first three words I think of to describe who I am are tenacious, optimistic and compassionate. I accepted Jesus as my Lord and Savior as a teenager and He changed my life. In my early 20s I answered God's call to ministry and became a licensed minister in 1995. I have been married for 28 years and really enjoy being married to my husband. I am the mother of 3 adult children, 2 adult children-in-laws and a grandmother of two. Being a mom and grandmother (GG) has been so rewarding. I love and appreciate my family. I thank God for the blessing they are in my life. Through ups and downs they have succeeded and I am godly proud of each one of them.

I experienced hardship very early in life. At the age of 10 my father was murdered. At the age of 12 my mom had a stroke and died. Then at the age of 14 my eldest sister was also murdered. It was only through the grace of God that I could go from tragedy to triumph. As a woman of purpose I have a passion for serving people and bringing hope to others. The struggle of the loss of my family has also given me a passion for the family unit which is why family means so much to me.

As a manager of practice development for a health and wellness company, I use my unique gifts God gave me to impact my circle of influence for His purposes every day. My role involves consulting and partnering to enable effective and prosperous practices. Our mission is to provide life changing personalized preventive care so people can lead healthier and more vibrant lives. It is a joy to be a part of making a difference and putting a smile on others faces.

You are called to be 'the salt and light' in this world. How do you see yourself fulfilling that command by working in the marketplace?

I believe in leading by example. When you are salt and light you will bring out the flavor of the abundant life and remove the darkness when you walk into the room. When I visit the practices in my territory I quickly realize all of us need an encouraging word and I am glad to be able to encourage and comfort others. Like Jesus, when you take the time to listen to people and get to know them, you make them feel important and what they must say is important.

I always remember the quote by Mary Kay Ash, "Everyone has an invisible sign hanging from their neck saying 'Make me feel important' Never forget this message when working with people.

How do you structure your time to reflect all the priorities and opportunities God has given you to be a light for him without losing yourself in the process, both personally and professionally?

I have found good time management is critical and so I have a color-coded calendar that keeps me focused, balanced and on track. I make time for the Lord, my husband my children, grandchildren, personal health, and professional responsibilities. If I am not careful I can easily fill my calendar with professional responsibilities at the risk of losing myself in the process, therefore I have learned to prioritize and my color-coded calendar helps me stay on track.

For example, my extended family and friends know when I am truly on vacation with my family I do not answer the phone or check emails. I have this time blocked out. When my three children were, small I would put family time on the schedule daily and it was not to be disturbed. Now that they are grown it is our vacation time together and we have our bonding time over family discussions and family game time.

In the same manner, I have created my personal time in my schedule. I have realized to be a light I must be healthy spiritually, physically, mentally, emotionally and financially. I schedule prayer and devotion time, workout time, spa time, pajama day, quiet time and I am glad my husband encourages me to have personal time often. Likewise, we have our couple time and it is so important. We do a getaway every quarter with regular dates in-between.

As a woman of faith, how do you integrate biblical and spiritual principles into your work environment with grace and truth?

I am blessed to work with people that understand the importance of a healthy spiritual life. It all works together. Our physical health in many cases is related to our spiritual health. Our inward and outward environment sets the course for our life. Therefore, because we are a company and people of integrity we care about the whole person and truly desire they live happier, healthier and vibrant lives.

Everyone needs a "Sabbath Rest". Even God rested after the six days of creation. How do you create space to recharge, refresh, and refocus?

In my weekly calendar, I schedule personal down time on Sunday. Every 5 to 6 weeks I schedule a week to focus more on administrative duties and I take that weekend to do a staycation. My beloved pajama day. I learned this secret from my spiritual mom.

She always had so many projects and a wonderful spirit of excellence and I always wondered where did she get all the energy to get it all done. One day I asked her and she told me she takes a pajama day. It is a do nothing but relax day or it can be more than a day. We all need it. As a minister, Sundays are work days and so we must sneak in some just plain down time to recharge, refresh and refocus.

As a woman of faith, what has been your biggest obstacle or challenge in the workplace, and how did you navigate that successfully?

As a woman of faith my biggest obstacle or challenge in the workplace has been to freely minister the gospel. We live in a world where we must be careful not to offend. Therefore, how I have been able to navigate through this challenge successfully is to make myself available for agreeable prayer and when able I share the daily bread devotional to help uplift someone in the workplace.

Have you ever felt 'guilty' for having a career or working? How did you resolve that, and where do you find mentors or support for your journey?

Absolutely, mainly while my children were young and I tried to balance it all. It was very hard work. I had to constantly refocus and realign my priorities. Now that my children are adults I now face the challenge of traveling for work and I am away from my family often. It is a lot to juggle but I am confident the Lord has placed me in this career for this season of my life.

I was able to resolve the guilt that is accompanied with being a working mom by a great book titled- A Working Women's Devotional When Every Hour's A Rush Hour by Christine Bolley and Jann C. Webster. I have been able to resolve the guilt of my traveling career that takes me away from my family by knowing it is a calling. It is also good training and preparation for my future ministry endeavors. I understand I am developing a skill set that will help me in building the Kingdom of God.

In addition, I understand from the teachings of evangelists like Billy Graham and Ravi Zaraias who were and are often away from their families for ministry it is a sacrifice. Many times, they were away from their families and Ravi spoke of tears in his eyes as he laid on the bed in his hotel room at night. However, we remember this is God's work and we die to self and answer the call. It is the call on one's life that must be answered. In many cases, we may not understand it but we just do it in obedience. We must answer the question what MUST I complete before I leave this place.

How did you choose your career, or did it choose you?

My career chose me. I had an idea I would love to do what I do before I started. However, I quickly knew this was a fit for me. My career allows me to use my specific skill set perfectly. My career is very apostolic in nature and it is the calling God has placed on my life. I am humbled, grateful and blessed by it every day.

I started my career in sales which trained me in people skills. I learned the truth of Zig Ziglar's quote that says "You can get everything in life you want if you will just help enough other people get what they want". I love helping people and it naturally progressed into consulting. In my career path, I have had to refocus myself to seek God on what I want so that it lines up with what he wants for me and others in the workplace. His plan will and purpose remains my motivation.

If you could give your 'younger self' any advice on integrating your faith life and your work life, what would it be? Would you do anything differently?

Honestly, I am not sure how this has happened but there is not much I would do differently. However, I would suggest the development of an effective time management tool at the onset of your career. Specifically making time for alone time with God early each day. It is too easy for one to get too wrapped up in work and forget we have a purpose to fulfill. Each day we need to be so in tune to the guidance of the Holy Spirit. Asking God what are your plans for me this day. How can I be a blessing today? Taking the time to listen and then following his lead.

One other thing if it were up to me I would have continued in full time ministry. It is the full integration of faith life and work life. I would describe it as heaven. I really enjoyed being the youth pastor and education director for a wonderful church I attended in South Dakota. The old saying, we have heard for years is you do not know what you have until it is gone is so true. My family relocated to Florida and I said goodbye to full time ministry for a season. In retrospect, I would have liked to continue in full time ministry; however, I needed to take the career path that chose me so I could gain additional skills and talents on the journey. My goal is to return to full time ministry again someday. Due to my work experience I will be better equipped for what God has called me to do.

How has your work challenged your faith, character, or values, and how have you been able to resolve that without compromising?

Over the years, work has challenged my faith and character and I have learned your ministry will never be more than your character.

How we carry ourselves in the work place, at home, on social media reflects our relationship with Christ. People are watching and paying attention.

When you can make a difference in another's life just by living a life of faith even before speaking about your faith that is powerful. As it is said in the bible *"Then you will know the truth and the truth will make you free"*. *John 8:32*. When we can allow ourselves to be vessels of God that will bring the truth of the Word to others then they can be made free. Kathryn Kuhlman said it best. "God is not looking for gold vessels or silver vessels. He is looking for yielded vessels."

Some women feel 'less spiritual' when working in a full-time career. How do you develop your spiritual life amid a demanding work life?

I can see how some women feel less spiritual when working a full-time career. When you work 40 to 50 hours in a week, trying to balance a home life and serve in your church there is a struggle to have time to develop your spiritual life. My work time may have some flexibility in how I structure my day however it is very demanding. I have learned spiritual development, must be a priority. I like to use my time wisely. I try to start my day seeking him for his guidance and reading a daily devotion. I use my driving time, airport time and any waiting time to read or listen to spiritual development material. I have recently gone back to journaling before I go to bed which I find is a great tool to communicate with God.

What is your favorite scripture, and how has that influenced your role as a woman who works and walks by faith?

My favorite scripture is *2 Corinthians 10:4-6," For the weapons of our warfare are not carnal, but mighty through God to the pulling down of strong holds; Casting down imaginations, and every high thing that exalteth itself against the knowledge of God, and bringing into captivity every thought to the obedience of Christ; And having in a readiness to revenge all disobedience, when your obedience is fulfilled"*.

This scripture has influenced my role as a woman who works and walks by faith because this scripture reveals to me we are called to do warfare. Living a walk of faith that is not by sight but by his Spirit. This scripture tells me we cannot do this in and of ourselves, it must be through God. I understand from this scripture I am in the workplace on a mission sent by God. People need the Lord. People need salvation, hope, healing, restoration, peace, joy, and love.

This scripture specifically began to mold and shape me when I was a young girl in my 20s. I realized I needed to have a strategic prayer life. God wanted me to pray for specific people and specific needs and I sought him and waited on his guidance. I love the ministry of intercession. It is one of my favorite ministries in the body of Christ. Prayer is just so powerful! I love spending time in the presence of the Lord. The bible says in *Psalm 16:11," You make known to me the path of life; in your presence, there is fullness of joy; at your right hand are pleasures evermore"*. Being in worship with the Lord is such a sweet place; I just love all aspects of spending time with Him in prayer.

Lastly in this scripture I realized that it is very important to obey God. Just like in the movie War Room we see how we must be ready to go to battle for our loved ones, our marriage, our children, our brothers and sisters in Christ, and the lost. God has asked us to stand in the gap. Like Daniel we must go before the throne on behalf of others, our nation and other nations. It is the believer's privilege as it says in the bible in Hebrews 4:16," Therefore let us come boldly to the throne of grace, that we may receive mercy and find grace to help us in our times of need".

Learn more about Gale Gillespie

 Evangelist Gale Gillespie serves as minister interceding, teaching and preaching the gospel all over the nation. Gillespie has served as youth pastor, education director and family and outreach director for many years. She founded and served as executive director of faithful minds tutorial services to help disadvantaged youth and is gifted in business development.

Evangelist Gillespie was born and raised in Queens, New York, where she accepted Jesus Christ as Lord and Savior in October 1985. Gillespie attended O.M. Kelly Bible College in Hempstead New York. She married Minister David Gillespie and from their union have 3 children. They moved to Rapid City, SD in 1991 where Gillespie received her calling and evangelist license. She served in the ministry at Faith Temple Church of God in Christ under the leadership of South Dakota State Bishop Lorenzo Kelly for 12 years until her call to the panhandle of Florida in 2004.

PATTI ANN RIDGWAY

Tell us about who you are, your profession, and how you use the unique gifts God gave you to impact your circle of influence for His Purposes in the workplace.

Whenever I am asked to share any part of my story I always give the glory to God! I believe every step of my journey was pre-ordained by my Lord and Maker. I am a 60 year young mama of 5 beautifully grown children, a mom to 5+ grand girlies and a blessed and highly favored child of God. I was a successful real estate investor for 25 years, until I was granted a journey that took me way out of my comfort and control zone. At that point in my life, I was faced with certain challenges and prayed unceasingly for God to remove them. Through these trials, I realized, God wanted to change me. I learned that it is through our tests that we gain our testimony and when God doesn't change our circumstances He is looking to change us. After many twists and turns ,ups and downs, I have selectively settled into my network/referral marketing business, a divinely inspired profession for sure.

We are all blessed with gifts and talents which I believe are graciously given by God. His intention being, for us to use these to fulfill our destiny. My gifts of nurturing, compassionately caring, honoring my temple, sharing my experiences, my passion for personal and spiritual growth, have all been assets to be an influencer in the workplace. I use my gifts to grow teams of like-minded individuals who bring their unique gifts, their purpose and passion. I partner with grateful people, who cherish this chance to give back and influence others. As we bring our gifts, we are paying our blessings forward and leaving a destiny. I purposefully surround myself with people who share my values and who strengthens me as well. People of faith naturally exude hope, joy, gratitude and love. Just as Jabez prayed in his prayer, I ask for a life of abundant impact and significance for God so I that I can become a light to the world.

You are called to be 'the salt and light' in this world. How do you see yourself fulfilling that command by working in the marketplace?

In Matthew 5 13-16, we are called to be the salt and the light in the world. It is our Christian calling as believers. Salt is a seasoning and persevering agent, making things palatable, and preserving goodness. Will I be that salt in other people's lives? Enhancing and adding to their days? Could I be preserving His good words and works that I have come to know as truth? Could I be the tour guide, leading others to His Holy Word? To preserve His word and bring it to the marketplace to those who do not know Him is a blessing. What a wonderful purpose to enhance the lives of others, a divine appointment for sure. Helping people live life to the fullest, co-creating to enhance physical, financial and spiritual wellness is my mission in the marketplace. I pray I bring people to faith in doing this. Faith in their own God given talents and abilities, faith in a broken economy and world, and faith in people who walk alongside them on their journey.

As the light I am to illuminate His greatness and His ways. This requires me to be involved and effective in my home, my relationships, my work environment and in the world at large. It is through my work, my deeds and my actions that people see I am a Christ follower. I remember one of my pastors sharing with me how we all hold a lantern and the light only illuminates a small portion of our path. But as we follow in the light we grow and illuminate the path for others. If by chance our light starts to dim, we know we have veered off course. Small adjustments every day keep us in the light and on the correct path. It is in His light that we are called to our true destiny. I pray every day for people to see Him and His light in me. I believe this is the light He wants me to carry and I am extremely blessed in my profession to be His light to others.

How do you structure your time to reflect all the priorities and opportunities God has given you to be a light for him without losing yourself in the process, both personally and professionally?

Structuring my time to optimize my opportunities means beginning each day with time spent in prayer, gratitude and devotion. I believe this prepares me with purpose and passion. To be productive, I need to lean into His design for my life and plugging into Him and His word first thing, allows me to feel His direction and guidance. I also pray to be open and aware of the opportunities that await me every day. I can become too preoccupied with worldly wants and needs and at times neglect to notice the still small situations that present themselves throughout the day. Opportunities to be an answer to someone's prayer, whether it be a warm welcome to a nervous newcomer or a soft shoulder for a hurting heart. Merely praying for, and over, people is a cherished chance for me to step into His grace and mercy at any time.

I personally have an unexplainable passion for "feeding people" and I continually pray to see the need around me. People today are hungry, not only in the literal sense, but emotionally and spiritually as well. I pray I lean into this calling to serve however I can. I am blessed to be better equipped now that my children are grown, in optimizing my time with Him. Years ago, at 33 I had unexpectedly given birth to identical twin boys. I bravely brought them home to my 3 beautiful children who were 3, 4 and 5 at the time. Life became a whirlwind of work, worry, schedules and shifts. Looking back, I realize I did lose myself at that time and the threads of my sanity and my spirituality wore thin. It has been through these times, these tests in my life, that I can see all the miraculous ways He is my salvation and the only one who can see me through. Surrendering to Him each morning is what allows me to not only step into His light but to carry His light out into the world.

As a woman of faith, how do you integrate biblical and spiritual principles into your work environment with grace and truth?

I am blessed to be in a profession where I can share my faith, my hope and my belief openly. In serving people and building my teams I tend to attract those with the same heart so I am never having to weigh my words or hold back my spirituality. I bring Him into all my conversations and I am an open book regarding reading His!

As a coach, mentor, and teacher, I take His advice and wisdom on honoring my temple, building a healthy spiritual history and blessing people who are suffering. Two of the many books I have read specifically touched on this. They are written by Laurie Beth Jones, *"Jesus CEO"* and *"Jesus Life Coach"*. In the pages of her books we learn from the best on how to manage and motivate others by incorporating the principles Jesus used. What better personal trainer could we ask for? As I train every day to run His race, it is second nature to integrate His principles. It is the fabric of my being.

Everyone needs a "Sabbath Rest". Even God rested after the six days of creation. How do you create space to recharge, refresh, and refocus?

Through the years, I have learned to love and take care of me. When I take care of me I can better serve others. Those lessons involve learning to set boundaries and balancing all areas of my life…. mind, body and spirit. Whether we are stay at home moms, corporate moms, working from home moms or empty nesters in the workplace-initiating, integrating and perpetuating our spirituality has it challenges. In setting aside time to nourish these areas of my life and making my secular and spiritual lives one, my whole life becomes my ministry.

Refreshing, refocusing and recharging are so much easier now that I live my passion and purpose. What I do recharges and refreshes me and it keeps me focused on Him and it has also become much easier since my children are grown. In working from my home, I tend to do 90 minute increments and then take half an hour to focus on me! What that looks like depends on the day but breaking my day into manageable bites works. In those shorter breaks, I can exercise, go in my sauna, do some laundry, cook a meal, pray, read, knit, take a bath, or connect with a friend. When I have bigger chunks of time off I tend to head to the woods. There I mingle with my Maker. In His glory, I am serenaded by the sounds and sights of nature and I'm gracious for His generous gifts. I often say my church is the woods.

I also gravitate towards my children and my little grand girlies to get some of that youthful yearning for all things new and exciting. I am blessed to have all my children nearby so a daily dose of little ones does my heart and my head good!

As a woman of faith, what has been your biggest obstacle or challenge in the workplace, and how did you navigate that successfully?

I would say my biggest challenge with my current business was coming to terms with creating abundance and making a living by "leveraging people". I had no previous knowledge of the industry and did not understand the opportunity I had to create the same results for those people with whom I joined hands. My thinking was that I was making money "off" of others. It was not until I prayed for understanding and guidance and truly did the work to learn about the industry, the culture, the business model and the intention that God had for me with this venture; that I truly felt comfortable sharing my gifts. I knew that this was a chance for me to truly impact others' lives, physically, financially and spiritually.

The first few years was directed towards my spiritual growth and development. Every step I took lead me in the direction of pursuing this further and understanding that this was my divine appointment. From my pastors' messages, every Sunday, my Bible Study books, my teachers and mentors all took me a few steps further on this journey. They shined their light on my path. I learned that we are blessed to be a blessing and an answer to people's prayers. I learned that God doesn't call the qualified, He qualifies the called. I couldn't ask God to guide my footsteps if I wasn't willing to move my feet so I did the work to better understand.

That challenge became an opportunity for me. A chance to help people who may feel the same way and need a better understanding of my industry and what I do. Challenges are merely opportunities for growth. I have learned to seize them happily!

Have you ever felt 'guilty' for having a career or working? How did you resolve that, and where do you find mentors or support for your journey?

I can honestly say that I never felt guilty for working or having a career. As a self-employed entrepreneur, I could adjust and rearrange my schedule around the things that mattered most in my life, namely my busy family. I worked from home when my children were growing up and I believe this led to their strong identity, independence and wonderful work ethics. When my children were little, I had them all doing their own laundry by 10 years of age. They each had 2 daily chores per week and rotated through the list. There was no TV Monday through Friday and that made time for the more important things. I remember other mom's asking how I got all their schoolwork done and turned in on time. I would respectfully remind them that I did my schoolwork some 30 years ago, and this was not my responsibility it was my children's. If my children didn't turn work in on time or forgot something they quickly learned to be more responsible by having to handle the consequences. I truly believe this gave them wings.

Guilt and shame are never good motivators. Providing for our family, physically, financially and spiritually are good motivators. Adding to the bottom line of my family made us all stronger and more connected. It created teamwork and instilled a sense of accomplishment for all.

I am blessed that my current career still offers me the freedom to juggle my schedule. It has allowed me the opportunity to witness the miraculous births of 3 of my granddaughters. I could be with my mother in her final years and by her side as hospice, my family and I transitioned her home to God. It blesses me every day, with the opportunity to teach others how to create more time freedom so they too, can experience the joy of making memories doing what is most important for them. My work is not what I do for a living, it is what I do while I am living. I can contribute to and celebrate all the memory making moments that come with having a great big, beautifully blessed family and a fulfilling and purposeful career.

As for mentors, I think God strategically placed people in my life just when and where I needed them. When I became acutely aware that I was searching for more passion and purpose in my life the proper people began popping up. The law of God's attraction at its finest. As I became more concise with communicating my beliefs, faith and values I believe God provided others with the same conviction to be drawn into my spiritual circle. There were many teachers/mentors who would take me further on my spiritual journey, contributing to and co-creating my spiritual history. Many mentors in the network marketing arena appeared, ones who would equip me to share this gift I was given. These angels are essential elements in my arsenal, ones that I turn to often. They inspire me to pay my testimony forward.

I remember one day at the onset of my network marketing journey meeting my friend Carol. She had just finished writing a book and she graciously shared it with me. I had no idea that day, that this chance meeting, while getting a pedicure, would change my spiritual journey forever. She has been salt and light in my life and on my Christian walk. Our similar paths bonded us in unimaginable ways and she is just one of the many spiritual souls He has blessed me with over the years. Keep your eyes, ears and heart open because He places angels everywhere!

How did you choose your career, or did it choose you?

I love to say that my career chose me and I share my story openly. Looking back at all the twists and turns I can clearly see it. However, as the tapestry developed, I had no clue. After my 24-year marriage ended I decided to go back to school to get my degree as a pastry chef and began my small business, Patti Cakes. Starting over in school and in the workplace at 45 wasn't easy but I felt this was where I was being led so I prayed and persisted in making a living, and creating a new life. I loved the creativity. Cooking and "feeding people" was always my passion but I continued to feel this hole in my heart and I knew down deep that this was not God's plan or my passion and purpose. So, I continued to pray unceasingly, as the bible so wisely advises.

It was in the spring of 2010 that my prayers were answered. I had inadvertently hurt myself while getting ready for church one morning and was laid up on the couch for well over a week. I ran into another angel I believe God strategically placed on my path. It was an old friend who I had not seen in 45 years. Deb just radiated health, confidence, love and light, everything I was praying for. So, I asked her what was her secret sauce, not knowing that she really would offer me a solution to my situation.

She shared how she and her husband Tom, were supplementing their fork and knife food with this superfood nutrition; which they had learned about from her sister. She also told me how it was impacting their health, their relationship and many other people's lives she was sharing with. Of course, I did my due diligence because honoring my temple was always a priority. I was still suffering with some inflammation in my body which I am sure was due to the stress and anxiety I still had circulating. I prayed and was still long enough to hear His voice. That voice of truth that had me step into the direction of His calling. That little lantern was lighting my way. This was truly how the good Lord placed my current profession on my plate.

I share this story with everyone because I believe there are no coincidences. I look back and see His hand in all my journey and I share that it is through my faithfulness that He answered. It is through my taking each next step that He continues to guide me. We are everyday people looking for solutions to issues we are challenged with, so we can live extraordinary lives. I believe God wants this for all of us.

Through all this I have developed a "give back" portion of my business in which I teach people how they can be paid to feed the hungry. Yes, that is right, I am in the business of feeding people! I truly feel my Project Feed It Forward ministry was also a divine appointment. I had been with my company for 4 years when I heard God say "feed people" as I had handed a homeless man a meal replacement bar. I have learned when I hear the voice of God, I listen! So, I now utilize my company as the vehicle for the wonderful nutrition (product), for the distribution of product and for compensation. I truly teach and mentor people how to be in the business of feeding people. I am most passionate about this leg of my business because I feel true success is in knowing God and living His mission for your life, loving all souls as your brothers and sisters and seeing their needs. My satisfaction comes from opening my arms, embracing and including others, so change can happen. In this way, I feel I serve the world at large. I believe we all want to be part of something bigger, something better, and something Godly inspired. We all want to feel as if we are making a difference.

I love the impact I have when I lock arms and move forward with others who are committed to doing His good work. This is when I know He is guiding my footsteps, when I work to accomplish what He has put in my heart. When I do my job, God does His.

If you could give your 'younger self' any advice on integrating your faith life and your work life, what would it be? Would you do anything differently?

The only advice I would give is the advice that I follow and that is to pray unceasingly, have faith, knowing that God's perspective is so much bigger than ours. I knew He was taking me on a journey and He was using me how He saw fit. I kept listening to the still small voice that kept pushing me to a greater purpose. It wasn't always comfortable but my faith and prayers kept me going and continue to do so.

I would not change a thing. Could I say I wish I had never put my family through a heart wrenching divorce, unraveling that fairy tale marriage and disrupting my children's lives? Do I question whether moving an hour away after my children were out of the home was the best decision? Could I say I married the wrong" person for me? Did I "waste" (what seemed like) years of my life in indecision searching for passion and purpose? Maybe, but life has evolved into something much more meaningful and beautiful in the last 14+ years and I wouldn't be who I am if I hadn't traveled this path. So, I tend to live in the testimony part of my life now and see the tests as the times of growth and development....my spiritual history so to speak.

How has your work challenged your faith, character, or values, and how have you been able to resolve that without compromising?

I feel my current work has not challenged my faith, character, or values in any way. Conversely, I feel the blessings in these areas of my life have grown as I have grown personally and spiritually on this walk. I can step into my purpose with passion and faith and live out every day in accordance with His plan for my life.

As I journeyed through the previous business ventures in my life I see how I was challenged and that lead me to keep searching and praying. I had been living in the shadow of what others wanted and expected for my life. I was not able to be my authentic self. It wasn't until I did the work, and walked through the pruning stages, (some of which were very painful at the time) and developed my spiritual history that the pieces of the puzzle began to come together for me.

I have had people comment on the validity of me being so open about my faith in my business and I share with them that is who I am and to be anything less would be inauthentic. I want to partner with other believers. That is the breath of my business. It is what gives us life, hope, passion, purpose and the faith, knowing that we are doing His work.

Some women feel 'less spiritual' when working in a full-time career. How do you develop your spiritual life amid a demanding work life?

As I mentioned earlier, I think when there is no distinction between our secular and spiritual lives the day to day become easier, more purposeful and our lives become our ministry. Incorporating my spirituality and doing His work by doing mine keeps me grounded and focused. Whether I am mentoring on honoring your temple, teaching how to create financial abundance and time freedom, or showing how to feed the hungry: it all revolves around loving others, being of service and lifting them up. In ministering to them, hopefully I am a link in the chain that brings us all closer to knowing, loving and serving God. A great book on this subject is Marianne Williamson's *The Law of Divine Compensation*.

What is your favorite scripture, and how has that influenced your role as a woman who works and walks by faith?

My favorite scripture is one that God shared with me at the same time He blessed me with this business opportunity. It has been on my website, my e-mail, my social media sites and on all my correspondences for the last 6+ years.

"Do not withhold good from those to whom it is due, when it is in your power to do it." Proverbs 3:27

This verse reminds me that God has empowered and entrusted me with specific gifts and talents to fulfill this mission. He has equipped me with everything I need to live His purpose for my life and fulfill my destiny. When I declare, and share my testimony of what God has done in my life, there is a power that is released into others that can make similar miracles happen in their lives. Every person exposed is a prayer answered. I have the power through Him and it is in my hands to give to others.

Now at 60 as I travel into more unchartered courses in my life, I am eternally grateful for my continued walk with Him and the healing power of prayer. My thoughts of my life's lessons, and how they are overflowing to future generations brings me peace and pride. I pray my fundamentals forever form that safety net for my family, friends and co-workers who follow in my footsteps. I have no doubt that *"praying unceasingly", 1 Thessalonians 5:17* was also my lifeline; the lifeline that this been my spiritual salvation. It continues to guide me and bring me back to all that is good in life. The gifts that are always present and the blessings that will continue to come. This verse has taken me throughout my entire lifetime- a lifetime of parenting, grand parenting, partnering, teaching, training and mentoring. So never stop praying, for God hears and heals when women pray at home and in the marketplace.

Learn more about Patti Ann Ridgway

 I am Patti Ann Ridgway, a faithful, blessed and highly favored child of God. I am the proud mama of 5 grown children and a mom-mom to 6+ grand girls. I am passionate about my family, my faith and feeding people...feeding people in the truest sense of the word. I co-create with ordinary people on a physical, financial and spiritual level so they may live extraordinary lives and pay their blessings forward. My life is driven by my God given purpose to "Withhold not good from those to whom it is due when it is in the power of my hand to do it." Proverbs 3:27

VICTORIA SOTO, JD

Tell us about who you are, your profession, and how you use the unique gifts God gave you to impact your circle of influence for His Purposes in the workplace:

I am a wife and mother, living in the great state of Texas. I have been married to my husband, Jerry for 15 years. We have a beautiful blended family, starting with our youngest son, Cristian who is such an awesome young man, on fire with the love of God and are blessed with amazing adult children, who have families of their own. I have been very blessed to have been a practicing attorney for the last 20 plus years. I have owned my own practice for more than 15 years of that time and have been blessed to have had my first book published and nationally released in 2016, "World's Best Doctors". God has always been a part of me. I have never been one to compartmentalize my work from the core of who I am, being a child of God.

From a very young age, my love for Christ blossomed by first realizing His profound love for me. His sacrifice on cavalry struck me so profoundly as a young girl. I recall declaring to my mother how excited I was at the thought of being in Heaven with Jesus. She, of course, told me that this was a beautiful declaration but that she wanted me with her a little longer and that she was sure that God had work for me to do on earth for the time being. . I was dubbed as a peacemaker early in life and that led, in great part, to my becoming an attorney, fighting for justice and freedom. To help those in need, to defend those who could be defenseless, to protect the rights and freedom of others, as God would lead them to me to do so. Understanding that this was my career path, I prayed my way through. I always say, pray in all things, through all things and for all things. Pray in faith and watch how God will move.

I am so very blessed to be a wife and mother and own my own business (law practice) which I have declared from day one, to be a "faith based practice". In my work, I have seen God's hand by taking what was deemed impossible and hopeless and because of God we are victorious.

You are called to be 'the salt and light' in this world. How do you see yourself fulfilling that command by working in the marketplace?

Along our way in this life, no matter the vocation or mission, we will always run across dark places. These dark places, could be the workplace where the environment may not lend itself to being Christ like. It could be the nature of our work and what it entails or the people within this workplace. Unfortunately, some will take this type of dark situation as a reason to flee, to quickly look for another place to work. Many times, you will hear our sisters or brethren state that they need a new place to work because they are called to surround themselves with Christ like people. Since these kinds of individuals seem to be void in their current workplace some of us may feel that they have the perfect reason to leave. Certainly, we are called to be with Christ like individuals.

However, we must remember that we, are called to be fishermen of men. To bring the lost to Christ, to guide the way, and to be the "salt and the light" in the work place. If we abide by this calling, then these "non-Christ like" individuals could then have what they need to become Christ like and if that becomes our reality in this place of work, then we will be abiding by what we are called to do as Christians. We will find ourselves surrounded by Christ like co-workers. In the marketplace of my business, which is all about protecting healthcare professionals, I find that when these very powerful people find themselves facing impossible odds and begin to lose hope and strength in whatever their fight maybe, I find, that the strength that I derive through my God gives me what I need to provide that salt and light to them. Whether they believe in God or not, their attorney does and I pray for them.

When I am told that a case is an "impossible case", because of who God is in my life, I get excited and feel a sense of great calm. This calm comes over me when I remember that it is not about me at all. It is about who God is in me and what He will breathe into any impossible situation that I may encounter. My God loves the "impossible". When others declare that a situation is "impossible", I say in prayer and declare that God loves the impossible because when the victory comes, then there is only one place to lay the glory in front of and that is our Lord Jesus Christ, Our Lord God.

With the victory comes their light. With this light in the victory of my work, I have heard clients declare and praise His name, who already know and believe in the Lord. I have also heard from those, who do not count themselves as believers, say to me that "maybe there is something to this God that you believe in so greatly", because of what they witnessed in seeing the impossible come to pass.

How do you structure your time to reflect all the priorities and opportunities God has given you to be a light for him without losing yourself in the process, both personally and professionally?

Wow, that is a difficult one to answer. It has always been impossible for me to separate who I am in Christ and who I am in my work. Maybe it is because my job is so complex and demanding that I am calling on my God for help and provision all day every day that I cannot see myself as being lost. One could say that work in general can be so demanding that we neglect ourselves by not having enough "me" time. However, I see my work as a big opportunity that our God has given me to do work for His Kingdom.

We are all called individually by our God to do a good work for him in the purpose and mission of our lives, whatever that purpose or work maybe. In my purposeful vocation in life, as an attorney, I find that if I do my work correctly and protect those, who are put in my charge to protect, then I am doing a good work for my God. Because we are all children, I am, taking care of God's children in serving my clients to the very best of my ability. Protecting my clients trickles down to their office, staff, and in providing for their families. Since I represent healthcare providers, if I protect them and allow them to do what God created them to do, then they will continue to be the best that they can be for the patients.

As we know, in their line of work, doctors are often in the position of saving the lives of their patients, improving their pain, thus giving them a better quality of life. So, considering the gravity of my clients work, if I do my part in being the best attorney that I can be for them, then we are all blessed in doing a good work for God. We are all part of our God's great work. If we all do what we are called to do by our Father God, then imagine what greatness will follow.

As Christians, we rely on each other to achieve and come into the blessing that God has for each of us. Therefore, we should uplift our sister and brethren in their calling. I do not see myself getting lost by prioritizing the opportunities God has given me because to not do this would risk true desolation and being separated from my God. It's an alternative that I do not have as an option. It is hard, it is not easy, however, it is blessed because of Him. Our God stands on His promises. There is no safer place to be than to walk in the path that He has laid for us.

As a woman of faith, how do you integrate biblical and spiritual principles into your work environment with grace and truth?

Biblical scripture and spiritual principles is how I run my business. We have all heard that if we stand in truth then we can never be tripped up on it. When people build their houses on deceit or on a principal that is not founded in scripture and the Word of God, then they have no true foundation. What they have built will eventually fall.

When I first decided to go out into private practice a few colleagues, working in different fields of law, considered to be bedrock and safe asked me if I was "off my rocker" to risk going into private practice all by my lonesome. As scary as it may have been, God put wonderful people in my life to show me the way and be a light for me in what could have been a dark time of transition. Still, the questions like "what possessed you to venture this way", the declarations that "you will never make it", would come up from time to time. In response to all this, I always had one answer, "My Lord Jesus Christ will provide and He stands on His promises".

While standing on His promise, I declared that my work and practice would be dedicated to God. With every new client I received I would praise God. Each new client was and is a blessing. People, who come to know me, quickly figure out that I am a woman of faith. Whether my clients believe in God or not, I always pray for them, whether they know it or not. I respect everyone's individuality and like Jesus, I never shove my faith down anyone's throat but I try every day to lead and behave towards others with love and respect and that is leading by example.

When asked about what fuels me, I am frank in my response and state that my fuel is my faith in my God. The old spiritual song, "They will know we are Christians by our Love, by our Love..." I am not sure if it is a title or a verse but that resonates with me. I am also blessed to have an amazing and supportive Paralegal, who believes in God and has great faith in Him. I find that it is wise for me to start each day in my prayer closet, reading scripture and thanking the Lord for blessing me with another day. This morning my prayer was that he would give me the strength to do good in the world in His name.

Everyone needs a "Sabbath Rest". Even God rested after the six days of creation. How do you create space to recharge, refresh, and refocus?

This is so very important. Being a woman in the business world today is constantly challenging. Many business women are wives, mothers, sisters and friends and devout church leaders and/or faithful elders, and that is a lot to contend with. Just running a company alone can break a person, let alone adding all the other titles that we carry on top. I personally carry all those titles and am so honored, blessed and humbled to do so.

For my time for rest, I do not know if it is an actual full day. Normally on "Sabbath Rest", I am in church, going to church or feeding people, being in fellowship with family and friends after church or my husband and I are getting our child and ourselves ready for school and the work week on the Monday following. I know that those of you in the same situation are saying "Amen" about right now.

How do we recharge, refresh, and refocus? Well, as a wonderful sister in Christ said to me years ago, just say this mantra "Just Jesus" and take a few deep breaths. I will tell you, my recharge is a quick one every morning with a prayer for strength, in my prayer closet, which can be in my actual clothes closet, or in the little prayer closet in my bathroom, where there is a "scroll" roll of paper nearby. Please note that I must always interject a level of humor and realism. That little prayer closet, can sometimes be the only place where a busy Mom and wife can get the most peace and quiet to pray and reflect and recharge, Amen! This statement, requires another "Amen".

I do try once every two months to unwind by treating myself to some quality time by going to the movies and seeing a "chick flick"-(romantic or epic film), if I find that there has been one of that nature released. . However, I have found that my most favorite way to recharge and refresh is by spending quality time with my family and friends. I, especially find it a great recharge and refresher to spend time with my fellow sisters in Christ. When you can find yourself a group of women of faith to spend quality time with, it is truly a blessing and rejuvenating. Sisters in Christ need one another. We gain so much from one another.

As a woman of faith, what has been your biggest obstacle or challenge in the workplace, and how did you navigate that successfully?

I would say that one of my biggest obstacles was one of my first experiences in private practice. I was blessed to be offered an opportunity to work in the private sector and bring what I had learned working for an agency into the private realm to assist doctors to be better at their calling (work), based on what I had learned to that point. In getting this new job where I had been promised a much larger salary than I had ever earned to that point.

I believed that getting this particular job was an answered prayer. However, once there, I found myself facing a large challenge that thankfully, I immediately trusted in the Lord to see me through when it presented itself. My new employer had offered me a dream salary if I would come into his firm and create a new division to defend doctors, not in the usual field of mal-practice, which is what people generally may think when it comes to healthcare attorneys, but in license defense. Doctors are generally used to the idea of one day facing a possible lawsuit in their careers. However, when their license to practice medicine is in danger that is when my work comes into play.

I felt comfortable defending doctors and assisting them in getting out of trouble and advising them on how to stay out of trouble, once the issue was resolved. I felt particularly comfortable because, up to that point, my work was to prosecute the licensed doctor and be a part of disciplining them, which affected their license to practice medicine. I was excited about the idea of protecting doctors and helping them, as opposed to prosecuting them. I hoped that through my work with them, they would survive a difficult process and come out better doctors at the end.

The prospect of this new job was so exciting. It promised me a great salary and a great office with a view. I was on my way to doing something good and to making a good living while doing it. On the very first day, I was told that one of the pivotal points in my accepting the job was no longer part of the deal. The person that was telling me this made it seem as though it was never part of the "deal". This individual was the very person who made the promise, which led to my accepting the job and resigning from the other job. When I was told that this very important point did not exist, I was, for a moment, struck with disbelief that this could be happening.

Then, praise the Lord, I was hit with the feeling that this individual believed that my resigning from my other job put me in a vulnerable position, where I would have no choice but to accept things the way they were. This person believed that they had all the power over my life. What this person did not realize was that I was not in that office listening to him alone. I had God and His infinite power with me. I looked into the eyes of this individual then I looked toward the beautiful window in his office and I called out to my God in my inner most self and prayed that the Holy Spirit would intervene and put the correct words in my mouth. In that moment, I spoke these words to the person in front of me. "Well, I thank you for the opportunity that has been given to me today. This is my first day and will apparently be my last day. The very thing that you have forgotten or say was never spoken was the reason that I took this position. I wish you and your firm great success and it has been a pleasure, however short." The shock that I would turn down such a huge salary and walk away with nothing was apparent. However, I had and still have faith in my Lord that "right" would be done by me.

A minute later, an individual walked and leaned in the doorway of the office and looked at the boss with one of her lovely eyebrows lifting at him. He cleared his throat and seemed to instantly remember the promise that he had made to me when I was offered the job and asked me to stay. It was a challenge to be brave and to turn down a salary that was triple that of the one I made the day before, but I knew that my Lord God was with me every step of the way and I braved it, only to be rewarded. Sure, you can guess that place could have been described as a dark place at times for me.

However, I decided to work in a place that I could have chosen to describe as a place of darkness. I was determined that God put me in that place for His purpose and to fulfill the purpose that He had for me. This is the belief that kept me going until God moved me on to another place. Through every step along the way, I knew, and have held on to the fact that I was walking with Him.... walking in the footsteps of Jesus.

Have you ever felt 'guilty' for having a career or working? How did you resolve that, and where do you find mentors or support for your journey?

Yes, I think that every mother, wife, sister, parent and child of somebody always feels that moment of guilt when they have a demanding career. Do not let the enemy lie to you sister or brother in Christ. You must hold on to the fact that to be the best mother, wife, daughter and friend is to first be the best you that you can be and who God called you to be. Having a career and doing what I do is what my God called me to be. Having a career may not be the most important purpose in my life, but it is part blessed purpose and part of who I am.

If I choose to be less than who I am, I will be short changing those that I love of all that I can be for them as well as for me. Some may say that to be in any leadership position, career or vocation that takes you out or away from home and family somehow reduces your value as a mother and wife. We have all heard these comments from time to time. However, you be, who God created you to be in every walk of your life. I do not judge those that would judge me for being a working mother and wife.

However, I advise them to embrace the situation that God put them in as I will embrace mine. My God has shown me the blessing of having a successful business, a healthy, well-adjusted, loving child, who loves the Lord God. My loving husband, is a strong leader and warrior for God and amazing father for our child. This is a testament to God and that I am alright in being all that I can be in my career.

How did you choose your career, or did it choose you?

As a prayer warrior from a young age, on fire for what was right, justice, peace and truth, I believe that my career chose me. I often reflect and refer to the story of our Lord and how He gave himself up, willingly on cavalry. How He was accused of crimes that He did not commit and He was without sin. Spotless and perfect. There has not been anyone like our Lord Jesus Christ. Praise the Lord!

When people say, how can you be a "defense attorney and defend "guilty" people? I say, my Lord Jesus Christ was the great defendant and He had no guilt. It is in honor of Him that I do my job every day.

If my client committed a fault in his work, then my client will admit it and endeavor to be better moving forward. I am blessed to have a successful practice and, for the most part, am in a position to choose who I defend. I am focused on righteousness and hope in whatever the situation the Lord God would have me in. Do your good work through God's grace, truth and love. When it is done through our Father God and by His will, you may know that "right" - will always prevail.

If you could give your 'younger self' any advice on integrating your faith life and your work life, what would it be? Would you do anything differently?

We have all felt fear, a sense of being inadequate in our abilities and trepidation along the pathway of our careers. It is only human and we are still on this plane of earth and not yet in heaven. The advice that I would give my "younger self" in those moments, that may have been fleeting, but still painful, is that when faced with these moments, speak the name of Jesus and I would remind myself that my Lord God got me through the previous trial, so He will get me through the next. Because God is the same, yesterday, today and tomorrow. His love is infinite and greater than we can imagine for us individually and personally. It does not falter when we do. Stay the course younger self and hold on to the Lord God, He has you.

I do not know if that would amount to changing anything along the way because what I have survived with the help of the good Lord has molded me into the woman of faith that I am today. Each challenge that I faced and survived I use today as a testament to His greatness and as a learning tool for my fellow Christians when the opportunity presents itself. I have been told that I have a parable for every scenario or a story that is relatable and that may be true. I believe that this is proof that God walked me through those situations, knowing that I would need them in the future for "a time such as this". If my experiences can help another than praise God!

How has your work challenged your faith, character, or values, and how have you been able to resolve that without compromising?

We all hear stories of how one professional does things differently from us. I have heard for years that I should be making so much more money if I were to only do this or do that, give less at the beginning to make more at the end. I have had bosses tell me that I hurt the bottom line because I won my cases at the lower level too often, thus taking away the opportunity to make more money if I would just give less and be forced to take a case to the "big show" (trial) where I could charge astronomical fees.

Well, my answer has always been that God does not bless that. I cannot give less than all that I have to a case from beginning to end. If that saves my client money in the end in legal fees that is great for my client and as for me, I will always hold fast to the fact that my Lord will bless me for doing what is right. You know what! God does bless His children! I have been so blessed by not taking the easy, compromising way. I have been so blessed by doing what is right and giving it my all from beginning to end. I may not be as wealthy, financially, as the next person that does what I do, but I am so blessed in the most important way and my God makes it so that people seek me because of the honest and caring way that endeavor to do my work every day as He would have me to do. Remember what I said about building your business on a strong foundation of

Godly righteousness. It is powerful and rewarding and my business thrives, praise God!

Some women feel 'less spiritual' when working in a full-time career. How do you develop your spiritual life amid a demanding work life?

Because I pray in all aspects of my work, God will bring the work to me. He brings His children together for His greater good, whether they know it or not. I feel more spiritual in my work because I pray and can see God move in it every day. Since it is demanding I call on Him all the time. We have heard of people finding "religion" in scary, demanding situations. When a person is flying on a plane and it feels like it is going to crash people who have not uttered the name of God in years, suddenly remember Him. Since my work is demanding, I am calling on Him all the time, so I praise God that I am drawn to Him daily in my work.

What is your favorite scripture, and how has that influenced your role as a woman who works and walks by faith?

I walk in faith every day with strength, confidence and courage knowing that my Lord God, Jesus Christ is with me. This knowledge leads me in all that I do. It is my stronghold and rescue, allowing me to make my journey on and receive what He has for me and mine. "Fear thou not, for I am with thee; be not dismayed, for I am thy God; I will strengthen thee; yea, I will help thee; yea, I will uphold thee with the right hand of my righteousness."

Isaiah 41:10 ASV "Fear thou not, for I am with thee; be not dismayed, for I am thy God; I will strengthen thee; yea, I will help thee; yea, I will uphold thee with the right hand of my righteousness."

Learn more about Victoria Soto, JD

 Victoria is lead counsel of the Law Office of Victoria Soto and concentrates her practice in defending physicians before the Texas Medical Board. She graduated from Southern University Law Center in Baton Rouge, Louisiana and was admitted to the Louisiana Bar in 1995 and the Texas Bar in 2001.

Beginning in 2001, Victoria served as a prosecuting attorney for the Texas Medical Board. During her tenure with the Board, she resolved a record number of cases, becoming a leader among her peers in case resolution and Agreed Orders resulting from administrative disciplinary proceedings such as Informal Settlement Conferences, Show Compliance Proceedings, License Committee hearings and State Office of Administrative Hearings/Mediations".

Since leaving the Texas Medical Board in 2005, Victoria has represented several hundred physicians before the Texas Medical Board. Her experience and extensive knowledge of medical board rules, procedures and policies coupled with her experience in working closely with board administrators, staff attorneys, affords her clients a seasoned and experienced representative before the Texas Medical Board.

Victoria speaks frequently to hospitals and medical groups within the State of Texas regarding the Texas Medical Board and its disciplinary process. She is a regular speaker and presenter for the Texas Medical Association at their annual TexMed conferences and other continuing medical education seminars throughout the state.

Victoria's first book was published and launched nationally in July of 2016. She is currently working on several new publications and is a keynote speaker for professional businesses throughout the country.

Victoria's law practice is located at 1005 S. Rock Street, Georgetown, TX 78626 and has a second location at 401 Congress Avenue, Ste. 1540, Austin, TX 78701. She can be reached at (512) 943-9284 or via email at victoria@vsotomedlaw.com.

LORI REESE PATTON

Tell us about who you are, your profession, and how you use the unique gifts God gave you to impact your circle of influence for His Purposes in the workplace.

I see the thread of God and the church throughout my life, even as my parents managed a trying relationship together. Our family moved 8 times to different cities and states between my first grade and middle school years. As an only child, I believe God gave me the independence and positive spirit to get on my bike or walk into a new school and be open to meeting new people. I sought it. I craved it. I wanted to be a part, to belong, to have connections. I suppose that is still a part of who I am today and has served me well in the workplace.

At age 11, I recall a teacher focusing upon our careers and possibilities for our futures. I can't explain it but I wanted to be something different- unique for women. Of course, I was coming from an immediate family where college had not been a priority but there was an expectation that I would attend one upon graduation. As the years moved on, I enjoyed science and math less and reading, presenting, and speaking more. The choice seemed to be clear- lawyer. Several teachers impacted my decision and I realize now more than ever just how important teachers are to informing how a young person sees herself. As I shared my goal with more teachers, I found that more of them confirmed my attributes to move in this direction. I loved to read. Check. I really loved to talk. Check (at least if I wanted to be a courtroom lawyer, that was a good skill!) I enjoyed writing. Check. Of course, I had no real idea what law school or practicing law would entail and yet I was hyper focused on this goal. It had defined how I saw myself and I never veered.

I attended a Methodist college for women, Wesleyan College, in Macon, Georgia. I excelled in that environment and challenged myself intellectually for the first time in my life. I had academic and leadership opportunities that were supported by professors with whom I had a real connection. I believe this is also a strength that God has given to me in terms of my personality. I literally have taken the Gallup StrengthsFinder Assessment and Connectedness is my 5th most prominent talent. That talent is defined as not only making connections between a variety of things to see the big picture and how things impact one another but it also has a spiritual component defined as believing we are all connected, part of something larger than ourselves.[1]

I attended law school at Mercer Law School, the Walter F. George School of Law, also in Macon, Georgia. Not only was I achieving my goal of becoming a lawyer but my personal connections in the Macon community had a tremendous lifelong impact that is alive today. I had interned at a local law firm in Macon with Albert Reichert. He was an amazing Christian man with a reputation of being the most and best of everything that a lawyer, husband, father, friend, citizen and human could be in this life. Connectedness and God's thread of protection appeared again. Mr. Reichert invited me to church and to their home for meals and special occasions. The Reichert's Christian love for me was very fulfilling and their friendship and mentoring of me have a lifelong imprint on my life. I learned that I didn't have to have the word God in every sentence to show my relationship with the Lord nor did I

---

[1] Gallup Clifton
Strengthsfinder*www.gallup.com/businessjournal/649/**connectedness**.aspx*Similar Clifton **StrengthsFinder** Theme. Things happen for a reason. You are sure of it. You are sure of it because in your soul you know that we are all connected. Yes, we are individuals, responsible for our own judgments and in possession of our own free will, but nonetheless we are part of something larger.

have to end every sentence with a reference to our Lord. He expressed in words and in his deeds that grace and mercy was key in this life and with people with whom we meet and interact. I can tell you that it took me a long time to implement his wisdom in my constant interactions with people.

I would have told you that I was a Christian throughout my high school, college and law school years. Of course, I would have said that I was a Christian in my early twenties. I went to church. I prayed. But my mind and heart were not renewed. I was not truly changed. I was (and still often remain) of this world while living in it. There are plenty of stories I could tell about poor choices in playing and casual partying during my college and law school years as well as my early twenties. I was no saint. More importantly, God's thread of protection remained a present force throughout these years through the people who loved me and continued to connect with me despite my human failings. Christian people were there; the church was there; God was there even if I wasn't yet ready to be a true believer and follower.

I met and married my law school sweetheart in 1994. Again, while there are stories here, I will say that we were friends and both had personal issues that prevented us from being a lifelong couple. This marriage and eventual divorce after only one year is an important catalyst to my becoming a believer and follower. I was still too young to fully understand myself much less all my family baggage that was not so neatly packed in my head and heart. I married intellectually- our relationship looked good on paper with our common law school background and generally being good, nice people. As we headed toward separation, I made the decision, out of my loneliness and suffocation, to have an emotional relationship with another person- in the workplace no less. Never good. Never ok. No excuses. At least he was single. But still not ok.

What was I doing? This is not who I saw myself to be. I left my first husband and launched into one of the richest and most fertile emotional and spiritual growth periods of my life post-divorce. Luckily, my two best friends from college were side by side as they watched me make poor choices. Through these friends, God was still there. They invited me to church and bible study; they showed grace and mercy not judgment. I was mortified. I couldn't admit to what I had done and decisions I had made. How could they want to be my friend? But they did and they showed me true Godly love during this part of my life.

I attended a women's retreat with them at a pinnacle point in my shame. I remember clearly that the leader was talking about the woman at the well. Jesus met her there. She was an adulterer and not the type of person who Jesus would hang out with- but He did. He showed that no matter what the person has done and no matter how wrong the action is considered by both society and God, Jesus does not abandon you. Jesus offers grace and tells us to forgive ourselves and be renewed. The retreat leader gave us bottles and asked us to put our sins and shame in those bottles and lower them into the well. Let them go. Really and truly release them so that they are no longer your baggage. In that moment, at that retreat, I felt that I had become a Christian. I wanted to be changed. I craved God's word and his time.

I was a criminal prosecutor during this time and my fellow prosecutors saw a change in me. Many of them commented upon it. My investigator used to laugh and tell me that I was tying up his Sunday school class with all the prayers going up for me. Now, he could finally move on to other people and other problems. So, funny and yet I clearly remember him telling me this over and over. It stuck with me and God was sticking with me. Once again, God's thread of protection and his people were with me and around me.

My faith in the workplace was more prevalent in my change in attitude and actions during those final years as a prosecutor. My nickname with many of the defense lawyers had been "Hellcat" for many appropriate reasons. As my time in that role ended, I found that my heart had started to soften and I started to see several my defendants as humans suffering in this world due to so many factors both within and outside of their control. I also realized that I had to move on from that role and that my heart was becoming jaded to the acts of violence I was surrounded by day to day. I didn't want to be that person and I knew my heart would be forever changed if I didn't take a break.

My next role was working for a telecommunications start up in the mid- nineties during the tech boom. I was flying high, literally, with constant travel and a new role that energized me. I also met Macon Patton, who would become my husband in 2003. Our relationship would help me to further define my faith and what I believed. We dated for several years long distance. Religion and my faith became a topic that concerned Macon. He wanted to understand my faith and how it informed my decisions. He saw my faith integrated into my life and he worried that he would not measure up. That was the crux. I was showing up as the Christian I wanted to be but would it cost me this relationship?

I recall telling Macon that I had to know that he was a believer, would attend church with me and raise children in the church. However, I did not expect him to meet my Christian faith or my relationship with God. I recall telling him that I couldn't get him into heaven; I could only give my life to God and increase my faith and Godly actions but couldn't take him with me. His faith, relationship with God and life choices in that pursuit would have to be his. Luckily, Macon worked through his concerns and we have had very meaningful and fruitful faith growing experienced together ever since our marriage.

God was using my talents in my career. In 2003, Macon and I moved to Charlotte and got married. I started a new role practicing law in a large law firm. It was going to be a very different role for me with long hours of research and writing; editing and perfecting; fewer hours in the courtroom where I had felt more fully engaged in what I enjoyed about being a lawyer.

I have experienced several life challenges in my present workplace, including infertility and, most recently, breast cancer. God was so good to me in leading loving support during my infertility journey. I prayed about how much to share with my mentors and supervisors. I chose to share what I was going through and seek support at work for the numerous appointments, tests, and procedures that we would go through during almost three years of the infertility struggle. God held me during that period with a church infertility support group and He gave me the confidence to know that whatever the impact of my honesty in the workplace, I was transparent in my life.

I felt God has clarified that wherever I was and whatever job I was doing, He was with me and would use me there. It is such a relief to know that I don't have to make a magic "right" decision in my career for God to use me. Our Father is a kind, generous, loving God who wants to give us so much. I suppose I understood this so much more when I had my own child and knew what it meant to be a parent- the immense love.

After the years of struggling with infertility, I had my son, Mac. He is an invitro baby and my only son. As his birth approached, I found that I was clearly not pursuing my passion in the countless hours of intellectual work behind my computer at the Firm. Once again, I chose transparency to share this lack of passion with trusted mentors and leaders while I sought to figure out what I would do after my maternity leave. I could clearly articulate what I believed were my strengths and skills while communicating that I couldn't leave this child and return to work without passion in my career. I prayed quite a lot seeking God's direction about what direction I should take when I returned.

I admit that I didn't find the daily mommy job of an infant (feeding, diapers, and sleeping baby) to be particularly fulfilling. I also knew that I did not find housekeeping particularly fulfilling. There are women and men who find housekeeping and infant responsibilities to be very fulfilling. My own mother felt that way. God has made us all with different passions, skills and desires. He has called us to different work. I went through so much to be a mom and wanted to be a mother- whether biologically or through adoption. However, the task oriented parts of motherhood weren't feeding my intellectual mind. As I continued to pray without knowing what the end game would be, I received a call about a new role that appeared to be an answer to prayer.

God confirmed He was at work as I spoke with the person who would become one of my main advisors and critical work partners. The woman partner and I had not known each other as we worked in different offices. I was once again transparent and told her that I had prayed about a career opportunity that would allow me to follow my passion for learning and people while also using my legal skills and other talents for the good of the Firm. It is important for our friends, significant others and employers to know who we are and who they are hiring. That's why I did not hesitate to tell her that I had prayed about it. I wanted her to know of faith and the critical role it played in who I was and who I would be at work. Her response? "Well, this must be a God thing because I have been praying about the right person for the role too." In the 10 years since that conversation, we have stood strong on our shared faith even though we have gone through challenging work situations and not always agreed. Our mutually shared faith has held us together at the end of the day to forgive, have grace and mercy, and show love.

Most recently I was diagnosed with breast cancer. Weeks before my diagnosis, I was driving in my car listening to Christian radio when the minister said" Have you asked God to use you?" Hmm. I had not done that. I asked God to use me in that moment but then said, "please don't let anything awful happen to me or my family'" Trying to put boundaries on God. Very funny. Almost as soon as I said this, I began thinking (or was prodded by the Holy Spirit) that my limits of God and fear of what could happen might be the devil trying to keep me from being used. Wow, if the devil could make me scared enough, then I'd never agree to be used through trust and faith. No way! I won't let that devil persuade me to be afraid and miss out on the opportunity to serve God.

Two weeks later, a diagnosis of aggressive breast cancer was confirmed. Of course, God knew this was coming. In the moment, I heard the news, I immediately went to that moment in my car. "OK, God. I know you will use this for your good. I am so mad but not at you. We did this with infertility and we will do it again." God had turned my mindset away from fear and toward the deal that we agreed to together in the car- God would use me for His glory. I am so thankful that he planted that perspective so that I could grab it instead of going straight to a place of panic and fear. This would be it and He had me. I also felt an incredible sense of peace. The peace that passes understanding just as the bible tells us about.

As our friends, family, neighborhood, school community, bible study, and workplace came together, I saw God's love pouring out over our entire family. Whether people brought food for months or sent their notes and scriptures, I knew God was prompting their love for a fellow believer. I was literally lifted to such a sense of peace through this journey with so much love. I have learned to be a good receiver as I see what people want to do to help me or my husband and child. I have said yes so much more to the offers that people have made and I am learning so many ways to serve others when I am on the other side of this journey. Weeks after my diagnosis, a young woman in our office recently diagnosed with breast cancer reached out to me. God was going to use me to encourage and pray for her. I would be able to pay it back sooner than I realized.

You are called to be 'the salt and light' in this world. How do you see yourself fulfilling that command by working in the marketplace?

The workplace culture can have so many constraints on people. There are many written and unwritten rules about how one should act or react in work meetings and as a part of a team. No matter what the "rules" are, we can commit to behaving in a Christ like manner. We can have interactions that display Christ's mercy and grace when fellow team members disappoint us or do things that go against the team structure. After all, our actions will show our beliefs much more clearly than just speaking about God or our beliefs.

Whether I am a part of a team or leading a team, I make conscious efforts to get to know people and understand what matters to them personally and professionally. As a leader, I have tried to think about my role in a servant's heart way. How can I give people opportunities, let go of my own need for control, encourage people to try new areas and support them if they succeed or fail? As a fellow team member, without a leadership role, I have had very conscious inner discussions with myself to be aware of jealous tendencies when a fellow co-worker received an opportunity that I really would like to have had. I have prayed about my own inner heart feelings and asked God to remove that and give me a legitimate heart for supporting that other person and hopes for their success. This is not easy and it requires us to be conscious of our hearts and attitudes.

We are the salt and light when we acknowledge all people in our workplace- no matter what their jobs may be. It is interesting to sit back and see how different people are treated simply because of their roles or their education. So many people are necessary to make our world go around and our workplace successful. We can never underestimate the importance and value of having eye contact and conversations with people who are the back bone to our organizations- a mail runner, receptionist, assistant, word processor, anyone who is seems to be somewhat unseen but critical to the workings of our marketplace machines. There is so much kindness and light we can bring to people.

How do you structure your time to reflect all the priorities and opportunities God has given you to be a light for him without losing yourself in the process, both personally and professionally?

No easy answer to this question! I look back and see that I have been on a bit of a roller coaster in creating and abiding by a successful structure in my almost 25 years in the workplace. There is no doubt that my commitment to a constant conversation with our Lord is usually happening when I am in the midst of personal and professional challenges. Isn't that always the way? We tend to go our own way when things are going well and when things are tough, we cling to our Lord. I am no different I'm afraid. Fortunately, or unfortunately, the Lord doesn't allow too many mountain top experiences to last for too long before bringing me back under his wing. But what if I didn't even have his wing or didn't know that I had the Lord to turn to in times of challenge, hurt and stress?

I live a full life and I love my full life. I have chosen to have a family and career, close friends and a community of activities. I must be intentional about my bible study groups and my prayer life so that I may grow and stay accountable to the Lord. I find that throughout my last 25 years, when I have been involved in a bible study- at my church or among friends, I am connecting with the Lord more often and I am learning and applying my faith to my life. I believe this is a critical consistent thing we must do as believers and followers.

I am also a believer in taking intentional time to get away and be alone. I admit that I am a bit of an introvert in terms of how I recharge- but I function very much as an extrovert. I need my time to either take a long walk, go to yoga, have a girl's weekend away, or go on a calmer vacation at least once a year where I can reflect and be more still. This helps me to take mental, emotional, physical, and spiritual time to realign with where I am and what I am doing. As women in the workplace, we must protect our time and allow others to do as much as possible for us if we can afford to do so- such as housecleaning, laundry, yard work- whatever can save us time and energy for the life we are building. Look at where you are spending energy and time and how much that really costs you.

As a woman of faith, how do you integrate biblical and spiritual principles into your work environment with grace and truth?

I have meaningful books or scriptures decorating my office to show my beliefs and who I am. We show our principles of faith through our actions and of course our words. I find that saying" I'm sorry" and tracking a person down to apologize when something has gone wrong is a way we can show our humility in the workplace. I don't find many people willing to say those simple words and yet they can have a big impact. I recall having a stern conversation with a team mate which felt uncomfortable to me. As I reflected on it, I felt that I had reacted too harshly. I called this team mate, made a date to sit down for lunch and came right out with it as we sat down- "I need to apologize to you." She seemed a bit shocked and curious. This conversation changed our relationship and made a good one even better. I know that she saw that the Lord was working in my heart to convict me and I paid attention to the nudge. Because she was a young woman serving my team, I felt that it was critical for me to show humility as a leader and for her to know that I respected her as a person and could admit to things that were wrong or things that went awry.

I also pray for God to give me the words to say when I have a difficult evaluation to communicate to someone. I let the person know that it is not an easy conversation to have but that it is necessary. I pray to speak with grace and truth but not with judgment or harsh criticism. I work hard to speak to the person and remind them that their work is not who they are. It is a job or a career that they participate in but they are a full person who may make mistakes or not be well suited to the work we must do. I always want a person to know that if they are not well suited to the work, there are other things and other places for them to find a home. Our work is not the end of the road and it is not a reflection on their worth in this world.

Everyone needs a "Sabbath Rest". Even God rested after the six days of creation. How do you create space to recharge, refresh, and refocus?

We must be intentional about our refreshing. I don't have much respect for those who are workaholics. I don't. Work Hard but live your full life. If your life is work, you are missing the mark. No matter what your work may be. I cannot claim to take every Sunday as a Sabbath and it is something I have been convicted of time and time again. But, I am a believer in refreshing in the way that meets your needs. We all need this refreshment and, in our culture, it is not always respected to take this time to replenish ourselves, our souls and our relationships. We must hold strong to the belief that this is important to a healthy, strong self and know that this is something called for by our Lord.

I treat myself to monthly massage and acupuncture as a true quiet respite that feeds my soul. I build it into my schedule as I would anything else in my life. I also build in times of retreat with my husband several times a year. A wonderful and wise counselor once told me to get away with my husband 4-5 times a year to keep our relationship strong. You don't have to go far- but you do have to leave your house. It doesn't have to cost a lot but you must get away. It requires intention and follow through.

I commit to seeing several different groups of women friends for that reconnection in our lives. It is a different type of refreshing my soul that leads to engaging our memories and learning more about who we are today. As a constant theme for me, it is the connection that we make on these annual trips that feeds me and I learn so much about them and myself. I can reflect on that connection and those interactions for a while leading up to the trip and for a while after the trip. We are much more fulfilled using our money and time this way versus buying a thing.

As a woman of faith, what has been your biggest obstacle or challenge in the workplace, and how did you navigate that successfully?

We can get very swept away by the culture of our workplace. I knew I had chosen a field that is highly stressful and has very high achievement expectations. I knew it but did not really understand it. The challenge has been to remain a healthy person- in all ways from physical and emotional to my spiritual life-while having such a demanding career path.

Health is a value of mine and it requires intentional effort to achieve or maintain some semblance of health in our culture. With only so many hours in our day, there are daily balancing acts that we are required to manage. I don't really like the word balance because it implies some 50/50 perfection which is never achieved for anyone. I think of it more as managing my priorities daily and knowing that every "yes" is a" no" to something else. With each important fact that we introduce into our lives, we must ask whether we have room to prioritize it in any way. If our personal and professional pipeline is so full with work, significant other, children, friends, and sleep, where will we find time for God and our spiritual growth? More realistically, we may find ourselves feeling very alone in even wanting this fullness of life if we work in a culture where people prioritize only work.

Have you ever felt 'guilty' for having a career or working? How did you resolve that, and where do you find mentors or support for your journey?

I have not felt guilty about having a career. Of course, I would not have felt this as a single person but I did not as a married person or after I had my son. I have spent much of my adult life working and work has truly been a part of who I am and my identity. I didn't realize until I had Mac and made a career shift that I had a lot wrapped up in my identity as a lawyer. Through my spouse, friends and mentors, I've been able to see a broader identity.

The mentors I've found have more often been through my bible study groups outside of work. Often, I have been engaged with evening bible study for working women and I find that there are so many more people like me attending those programs.

How did you choose your career, or did it choose you?

As I mentioned earlier, I chose my career as a lawyer from an early age.

If you could give your 'younger self' any advice on integrating your faith life and your work life, what would it be? Would you do anything differently?

Our faith life is integrated into our work life naturally if we are a faithful believer and follower of Christ. Our Christian life is our life. It is who we are and lacks integration because it is so much a part of who we are both spirit and soul.

Stay in bible study! I look back on how I fed my soul through the evening bible studies throughout my twenties and thirties and now in my forties. I believe those relationships in bible study and the discipline to stay in the word and accountable to others is what kept me continually growing my spirit and faith. As my faith grew, it became more of who I was and my mind was renewed. I didn't check my soul and mind at the door of my workplace. I was one person working to grow in knowledge and wisdom for parts of my life.

How has your work challenged your faith, character, or values, and how have you been able to resolve that without compromising?

I have had to be very strong and stay very true to my pursuit of finding my own healthy path while working full time in a professional services world. I must manage my mental state and this is where our faith is critical. Many times, I've wondered if I am seen as lazy because I call it a night when I must sleep or choose to wake up early to exercise instead of going to work early. No one has ever called me lazy, but after a few years of watching just about everyone else choose completely different paths from mine, I sometimes start to wonder. If I don't have a clear sense of who I am, meaning my values and priorities, then I could get sucked into a very unhealthy lifestyle. If I didn't know who I am in Christ (and pursue consistent learning about what the Bible says and who God is) I'd lack the confirmation to have those mental talks with myself reassuring me that I am living my life respecting all that God has given to me.

Some women feel 'less spiritual' when working in a full-time career. How do you develop your spiritual life amid a demanding work life?

I am a true believer in having a small group study as part of your disciplined Christian life. The wonderful part of today's world is that many of us can find an online bible study and not have to leave our homes at night to attend. We can attend bible study that meets at night so that we can be fully engaged at work and we can have our study time.

I read my favorite devotionals to start my day and have a perspective with which to start my day. Devotional apps like Jesus Calling or Streams in the Desert which are two of my favorites. These can be read or re-read during a break at work or as part of our lunch and offer perspective on our day. In this way, we refresh our thoughts and renew our minds even amid challenging workplaces.

Finally, attend women's retreats- whether that is organized by your church or simply gathering your small group or bible study and getting away for the weekend together with bibles in hand. Retreats can be very mountaintop experiences that offer us mental, emotional, and spiritual nourishment and relationships with other women as we grow in wisdom. Just as we need to get away for a vacation and refresh ourselves or our relationships, our spiritual life is no different. We need the change of scenery to refresh ourselves and gain new perspective which can be applied to our same old life and same old problems at work and at home.

What is your favorite scripture, and how has that influenced your role as a woman who works and walks by faith?

Romans 8:28 "And we know that in all things God works for the good of those who love Him, who, have been called according to his purpose." I am a glass half full person. I want to find purpose and connection for the things of this life and this world. Notice this scripture doesn't say that good things happen to those of us who are faithful Christians. This scripture doesn't say that only good comes out of all things for those of us who are Christians. It does say that God is working in all things – the good, the bad and the ugly- for the good of those of us who love Him and are called according to HIS purpose. Our "good" may be, unfortunately, to suffer for the kingdom and yet there is a greater purpose for our lives. We know we will live with Him in eternity so we can suffer here for that possibility that we are glorifying Him for other believers and non-believers to see.

Our lives ebb and flow through the valley and mountaintop but that's just it- it is constantly changing. We can count on the change. But within and through the change, God is our constant. His peace can really be had during so many things in this world. I have felt it and I know it to be true.

Learn more about Lori Reese Patton

 Professionally, Lori's career experience includes career criminal prosecutor, V.P. of Governmental Affairs for a telecom start-up and, most recently, as a practicing lawyer and, now, Chief Learning Officer for a law firm for the last 14 years. Lori has integrated of her faith and life through active participation in church and community. Whether a Young Life leader, Sunday school teacher, church sponsored infertility support group facilitator, Stephen minister, or breast cancer survivor, Lori believes that we can use our life experiences to show God's love and support of others. She is a graduate Wesleyan Women's College, a Methodist college, and Mercer University Law School.

BREN OLSEN

Tell us about who you are, your profession, and how you use the unique gifts God gave you to impact your circle of influence for His Purposes in the workplace?

Who am I? I am a woman who is passionate about hope and freedom to become all that God created us to be. I am driven to find, provide and be part of loving and encouraging environments, relationships and social situations that cultivate this freedom.

Being the youngest of five children had a major impact on who I am today. It was the first team I was ever a part of. My family was accepting, encouraging, inspirational and strong. We were not perfect and that was the perfect part. This team environment cultivated confidence and character.

I assumed everyone grew up this same way. I never even thought about it until much later in life when I noticed differences in people's reactions to the openness I was raised with. Experiences from the past or present made it difficult for some to be authentic, courageous and confident. It was as if they weren't free to be themselves and were resentful of those who were. They were chained to their fear of failure, criticism and past mistakes. Some lashed out with jealousy, gossip, and harsh criticism. Others were terrified to try new things, meet new people or make changes to live a better life. I was heartbroken over it. These experiences birthed my desire to spread the message of being freed from that which chains us. To assist in the transformation of becoming all God intended us to be. "To restore all the years that the swarming locust has eaten" Joel 2:25. I prayed for God to help me be an encourager, a beacon of truth and have opportunities to coach others in the process of becoming free. This is my ongoing motivation and passion in my personal life and in the workplace.

God gave this small-town girl, spiritual gifts of exhortation, faith, administration, discernment, leadership and shepherding. He gives us each our own blend and portion of giftedness. He also threw in a scoop of boldness and sent me on my way. It was hard work getting free from my own chains of the past. I needed practice in how to be strong and kind, speaking the truth with grace and learning to be led before I lead. I had to grow into being gracious, loving and gentle. Through the years, the Holy Spirit has tempered me to yield these things to His leading. Believe me I tried to do myself. Some work can only be accomplished on your knees in surrender.

God knows that I love challenges and innovative opportunities. He made me to be a builder and a dreamer. He sends me to people and places that are looking for this very thing. Not that they can't do it without me, but rather I can't do it without Him. I experience God this way. It deepens my faith and is a way He loves and leads me.

I consider myself blessed to have had co-workers, family and friends who have believed in me, saw my potential, spent their time and money training me and even incubated me when I needed it. I discovered God's plan for me to reach out within the church setting and outside of it. To love and live in the workplace.

You are called to be "the salt and light" in this world. How do you see yourself fulfilling that command by working in the marketplace?

Matthew 5:13-16 commands us to be salt and light. To go out into the world and sprinkle holy flavor around! Not to hide our faith but let it shine brightly everywhere we go. I liken it to being a field guide with a salt shaker and a flashlight. Shaking salt on and in situations and relationships so it tastes good. Shining the light on how to live an authentic life that isn't perfect but its goal is to please God.

I get energized being around other people. I want to enjoy my time with co-workers. Let's face it we spend a lot of time together. I am interested in their lives and want each of us to be successful. And shoot, if we can laugh and have a good time while we are at it that blesses me even more!

I don't hide that I need Jesus every moment of my day. I openly ask for Him to change my attitude if it needs it. I praise Him when things go well, even if it is something as simple as the copier working correctly. I feel that my job performance reflects my character. I want to do well. I show up on time and I try not to complain gossip or spread negativity. I welcome feedback and constructive criticism. Now, I don't accomplish all of this perfectly every day. I have been known to grumble a time or two or more. I have even had to humbly go back and apologize for doing so. I haven't always agreed with the criticism at first but I take a few days and ask God to show me truth in it. Usually, more times than not there was a thread of truth in it and an opportunity to grow and improve.

Praying for others is a huge part of being salt and light. I consider it a privilege to go before the throne, to be an usher into the Holy presence of God. I don't have to know all the details; I don't have to have numerous conversations I just simply offer. I hope they see Him in me and want what He has given me, a better life.

We may not always see how we are impacting the lives of those around us in the workplace. I surrender this to God. I don't look at others as an assignment but rather a connection and a blessing. I enjoy getting to know people better and sharing work life as we cross paths. Many times, I ask myself and God, really, this is what I get to do? God is good.

How do you structure your time to reflect all the priorities and opportunities God has given you to be light for Him without losing yourself in the process, both personally and professionally?

Like the old saying goes, time is precious. I am careful not to overextend myself or I can get frazzled and resentful. I have gone through seasons where my commitments were challenging. Especially when raising our children. I worked part time so that I could meet the demands of their and our schedules. Dinner around the table together, was a priority for us. Traveling for sports was a given. I don't regret that. I treasure those days. It was tough but we did it. Being a mom and wife has been one of my greatest blessings.

In the past, when I was in ministry leadership it could became demanding in regards to meeting expectations of others, accountability, and being available. If I wasn't careful it could take over my personal life. Many days I was giving work all my best and then found my tank empty when I got home. I longed for balance between these two areas in my life. I had to figure this out. Once again I was led to my knees, so much so, that it became a yearlong prayer. "Lord, help me to be as loving, eager, and available at home as I am at work. Narrow that distance and difference Lord."

The answer wasn't in reprioritizing activities or making adjustments in my planner. Yes, those things happened in the process but the balance came through discovering and embracing my identity and purpose. God taught me to not give of myself but to offer Him. That my time and resources had limits, but His didn't. His presence and power in their lives was the key, not mine. I started reading books about how other women handled all the pressures of trying to be super woman. I started learning more about my spiritual gifts and concentrated on what I was good at. I stopped trying to be all things to all people. I learned to say no. Eventually I hung up my cape and put on my crown. I knew who I was and whose I was. Life changing!

All I have to offer is Jesus and that's everything. He has the power to save, not me. The only walk with Jesus I am accountable for is mine. A huge weight lifted off my shoulders. Like a giant backpack filled with bricks taken off.

I now enjoy time with family, friends, myself and my workplace. My identity, purpose, success and failures all lay at the cross. Jesus gets the glory no matter what. My part is to be myself, obey and introduce love, life and the hope that Jesus provides. I may fall down, mess up or miss opportunities. That's ok. God is way bigger than me. He's got the whole world in his hands!

As a woman of faith, how do you integrate biblical and spiritual principles into your work environment with grace and truth?

The best way for me to integrate biblical principles at work is to remember that my actions speak louder than words. In my opinion I don't have to preach and quote scripture every day. It takes courage to be different and step out with an unpopular belief or action but over time you build a reputation for doing the right thing.

Common courtesy goes a long way in building relationships at work. Saying please and thank you is a simple way to show appreciation. I try to serve others by helping with tasks, volunteering for team building exercises, and organizing fun and food for social occasions. I enjoy helping my co-workers feel special and appreciated.

I find it's valuable to give grace when witnessing mistakes. I want to experience that same grace when I mess up. In today's world of finger pointing this speaks volumes. I am not saying we shouldn't hold others accountable for their actions, especially if it is in your job description to do so. I am referring to minor everyday errors, not handbook violations. It is very competitive in the workplace and extending grace offers a level of kindness and courage that others may not have experienced before. I enjoy passing out compliments generously. I love seeing others do what they do well. I have worked alongside amazing, creative, talented and gifted people. I can appreciate the time and effort involved in a job well done.

I own up to my mistakes and make it right whenever possible. I try not to compare personalities or performances unless my job description requires me to. I make great efforts to see potential and possibility in everyone. Seeing other's through Jesus's eyes. Above all else, spend time in the word so you will know how to speak the truth in a gracious way.

There have been times when I have had to tell hard truths, things that aren't popular or received well. It isn't easy but I have found that if my heart is in the right position, if I yield my mouth, my attitude to the Holy Spirit and if my motives are pure, to build one another up and not to tear down; I can walk away from the experience with a clean conscience and a good result.

Lastly, I am mindful of the fruits if the Holy Spirit listed in *Galatians 5:23 - 24. "But the fruit of the Spirit is love, joy, peace, patience, kindness, goodness, faithfulness gentleness and self-control."* I try to lead and respond with these qualities. My prayer is that others observe, find out my source and want it for themselves.

Everyone needs a Sabbath Rest." Even God rested after six days of creation. How do you create space to recharge, refresh and refocus?

Let me just say that I was wearing myself out trying to find rest. I kept thinking I needed to be left alone. I equated sleep and or naps with rest. I dreamt about being rested, I heard other women talk about it like it was a magic pill that would help us all see clearer, make us want to cook, clean, do homework, teach Bible study and organize the carpool schedule all at the same time. I planned for down time and guarded it like a bull dog. It makes me laugh now about how intense I was. Over and over for many years I would try to get rest. I just wanted a nap and then when I was alone, I felt guilty and couldn't sleep. Never accomplished it! Ever!

One weekend I noticed how rested I felt after binging on some Beth Moore teachings. I thought, hmmm funny I didn't nap at all this weekend and I feel great! So, refreshed! What's going on here? Where was this energy coming from? I took notice and was determined to find where this wellspring was coming from. I started journaling again, writing down thoughts and thankfulness about my day. I also took notes while watching speakers on TV and DVD.

I also wrote out scripture, you know those daily lists you can print out from Pinterest. I began to dig deeper into studying the word again. I recorded it all in my journal. Ok, honestly, my original motivation was to get my life down on paper for my children, grandchildren and their grandchildren to see. I wanted to leave a legacy, a memoir of Bren's life. Focusing on how exciting it was to walk with Jesus. I dreamt of future generations happening across my collection of writings like a treasure chest. True story! You can't make this stuff up! It was in these journal entries that I discovered the source of my new-found energy. It wasn't rest it was renewal, refreshment, and refocus!

I made a list of the things that made me happy and energized me:

- Making an effort to looking my best every day. Hair, make up the whole bit.

- Reading the Bible in my hands physically not electronically. The sound of those crisp pages turning soothes me.
- Cooking, chopping and planning healthy meals.
- Anything that had to do with my husband, kids and grandkids.
- Spending time with friends laughing and sharing even a couple hours together.
- Listening to others, I mean really listening without thinking about what my response is going to be.
- Being creative. Photography, drawing, painting, etc.

You get the idea. I started celebrating my life and my loves. I had more energy and zeal than any nap I ever hoped to have. Now I make it a daily thing to do what brings me joy, whatever that is, wherever I go. Seek out your wellspring!

As a woman of faith, what has been your biggest challenge in the workplace, and how did you navigate that successfully?

My biggest obstacle or challenge at work is not letting other's behavior affect my attitude or behavior. I battle the temptation to get irritated or ticked off. When I do, conversations pop in my head of things I would like to say aloud. If I am not careful, I do. I realize this is exactly where the enemy would like me to stay. To see people through his eyes instead of God's.

I have learned over the years not to let that hook settle in my heart or mind but get rid of its hold as fast as I can. I must react quickly to forgive or at the very least offer it up to God. Where my heart is, my mind will follow. If I let my feelings run with it I may end up where I don't want to go. Believe me there have been times that I have walked around with that hook in all day. I can't even talk straight when that happens. I may think it's hidden but it is clearly sticking right out there for everyone to see. Now, I go on a walk even if it's just to the restroom, and hand it over to God. When I return to my work area I am usually back on track. I try not to take it personally and get offended. Satan likes me to be offended.

I don't want to give a false impression that nothing bothers me or that I'm invincible and nothing can penetrate my mood. I simply don't want to spend too much time, energy or emotion on it. I don't want to pass on the negativity to those around me. I am supposed to be sprinkling salt and shining light! When I involve God in ALL situations, he will keep me on the straight and narrow. He lights each step I take and fills in the blanks.

I know I can trust Him with my feelings. I know it's always a good idea to be kinder than what I feel. There are usually lots of great things that happened during the day that I would rather give my time and attention to. I don't want to miss out on the blessings right in front of me because I am all sassy. I pull that hook out and toss it to God as soon as possible. I call it a catch and release.

Have you ever felt "guilty" for having a career or working? How did you resolve that, and where do you find mentors or support for your journey?

I don't feel guilty for working. The workplace is a natural way for me to express myself and cultivate my gifts and talents. My positions and opportunities have been within my spiritual giftedness and skill set. It makes work both enjoyable and fulfilling. Knowing who we are and how God has made us is key. It will bring us joy when exercising these gifts. Whether you stay at home, volunteer, work full time or part time (I have done all of them), where you are called is where you are called.

I am passionate about connecting with other leaders. I make community a priority. I have sought out groups locally, joined FB groups, followed leaders on Twitter and Instagram. I gather inspiration and support wherever I can. I know I need to stay connected and pull up to dock for fresh faith, views and encouragement. Staying connected to resources is essential for me to stay vibrant and strong in my walk, my field and my faith.

How did you choose your career, or did it choose you?

I didn't choose my career that's for sure. I don't know that I would categorize it as such. Here is a chronological list of the different genres I have worked in beauty industry, manufacturing, ministry, marketing and precious metal purchasing, back to the beauty industry and now retail administration. The common thread is being involved at the beginning of a project or the beginning stages at least. I am a builder of sorts. I love pioneering. I have built a reputation for bringing about change and new direction.

The cool thing is God knows how much I love a change. Ask my family about this. I am always moving the furniture and rearranging the closets. They did not appreciate me swapping out drawers in the kitchen creating a hunt for the silverware or napkins though. Ok I admit it, I tend to get bored. God knows this. I have taken baby steps and giant leaps alike, both equally thrilling and some more challenging. I love surveying the new territory and planning for the future. I feel absolutely blessed! When Jesus is the project manager, there's no stopping us!

If you could give your "younger self" any advice on integrating your faith life and your work life, what would it be? Would you do anything differently?

If I could give my younger self any advice about faith in the workplace, it would be to relax and chill out. I would say embrace the personality God gave you and trust yourself more.

Here are a handful of one liners I have used for many years now.

- Pray more than you say.
- Speak less and listen more.
- Go to the throne before going to the phone.
- Look at yourself in the mirror not through a magnifying glass.
- Filter those thoughts through the mind of Christ.
- Don't let anyone put a lid on your progress.

These are applicable to my life even today, timeless advice. Lastly, I would tell myself to slow down and be present for every twist, turn and acceleration God has planned. It is a wonderful ride! I wouldn't do anything differently.

How has your work challenged your faith, character, or values, and how have you been able to resolve that without compromising?

I fortunately have had very few challenges over my values and faith. This is an area that I am not afraid to be bold in. I am accountable to God for my actions and I will not compromise.

I have however, been exposed to poking fun at Christian values. Does it hit a cord with me? Yes. What do I do about it? It depends, most of the time I ignore it. By doing so I don't feel lesser than or that I am not honoring God because I didn't call someone out on it. I leave this task up to God. I try to let it roll off my back like water on a duck. It takes practice.

Some women feel "less spiritual" when working a fulltime career. How do you develop your spiritual life amid a demanding work life?

Work is a natural extension of me. My relationship with Jesus isn't part time; it is a full time gig for me. I take Him everywhere. I need Him every moment. I wake up early specifically to have extra time with Him at the start of my day. I read my Bible, journal or listen to podcasts while applying my make-up and styling my hair. I listen to worship music on Pandora or Alexa, anything that will help me focus on yielding myself and my day over to His plan. If you are in the season of raising your kids, worship music is a great way to start to their day too.

Once I am in the car it's more of the same. We have so many options available to us. I listen to Sirius radio; local stations, Pandora, podcasts, it all depends. I choose whatever will set my heart and mind on Christ.

Currently, when I get to work I have a devotional calendar I read at my desk. I ponder over it and say a short prayer giving my day to God. I usually have a verse or word on a post it note stuck to my desktop or monitor. These are words God has impressed upon my heart. It's in the mix of my other desk décor to have eye shot to help keep me on track and task. These are all things I can do under the radar. It doesn't have to be an outwardly flamboyant faith. We don't have to act like we are IN church. We just must BE the church. A smile, a touch, or listening ears are simple and easy ways to reach out to others. At the end of my work day, I call my husband to let him know I am on my way home and then the rest of my drive is a celebration. I made it another day. I crank the music and settle in for the drive home. All these things help me to plug in and partner with God.

I decided years ago, to stop striving for a perfect day. There are days all I can manage to fit in is my worship time in the car. That's ok. Tomorrow is another day. Our hearts desire is what God looks at, not our performance. If you are a driven person like I am, this may be hard to accept at first. We enjoy that feeling of crossing everything off our list. Ask God to redefine your day and your list. He won't disappoint.

What is your favorite scripture, and how has that influenced your role as a woman who works and walks by faith?

My favorite scripture is *Proverbs 3:5-6 "Trust in the LORD with all your heart And do not lean on your own understanding. In all your ways acknowledge Him, And He will make your paths straight."*

God gave this verse me during a difficult time of grief. I was in somewhat of a foggy place. I needed direction, I was sad and hurting. I needed His wisdom, guidance and understanding. I cried out to Him on a midnight walk and He met me there. Under the moonlight He held my hand, lit up the next step and I moved forward. He is gentle and strong all at the same time. He is faithful and gracious. He knows everything about me. He is trustworthy.

As organized and prepared as I like to be, my journey with Jesus has been unpredictable. He has walked me down paths I would never have seen for myself. He has reached out and grabbed me when I thought I would drown. He has asked difficult things of me. He has asked me to trust him even when I can't see past the current step I am on. Let me tell you great is His faithfulness. He is who He says He is and He can do what He says He can do.

This very scripture is what led me from formal church ministry into the workplace. I wasn't sure of every detail so I asked Him to light my way and He did. He lights my path one step at a time and fills in the blanks I can't see for myself. It's an adventure!

Learn more about Bren Olsen

Bren loves people. She has worked in several genres approaching each one the same. God give me your eyes to see people the way you see them. Help me to love others the way you love me. She has served in the church as a Preschool Program and Women's Ministry Director. Worked in the marketplace as an Office Manager, a Precious Metals Buyer, a Salon and Spa Manager, and is currently working in retail administration. She coaches others in finding hope in freedom to be all that God created them to be. Bren married her high school sweetheart Jeff 30 years ago. She is mom to Tyler and his wife Makenzie & Autumn and her husband Kyle. She is Grandma to Emmett, Atley and new arrival coming in July 2017.

DANITA SCOTT

Tell us about who you are, your profession, and how you use the unique gifts God gave you to impact your circle of influence for His Purposes in the workplace.

I decided to become a professional speaker for two reasons one because I could never imagine just one career choice for myself and because I needed to follow my own path in life. I always wanted to be one of these people with a perfect map of my career but my career map looks like a series of circles and highs in lows. My journey to this career was completely unconventional; in my short time of working, I have had over 30 jobs. I've worked as a professional makeup artist, in advertising sales, as a retail professional, a car salesperson, and in youth ministry. I had a hard time deciding what I really want to do with my life but along the way, I found a theme in all my work—I am an influencer. God has given me a lot of unique gifts but the one that is evident in my everyday life is what I would call influence.

I influence people to eliminate patterns of failure and perfection in their lives. Growing up, I was shy, awkward and not well spoken. I always wanted to do big bold things like act in plays and participate in pageants. When it was time to perform, I relied on my mom to help with everything. When I was a Girl Scout, I wouldn't even sell my cookies (my mom sold them all) because I was so afraid to talk to people. At that time, it didn't seem that I would have a career in public speaking, as it was not a part of my plan, but a part of my destiny.

I have spent the last ten years of my career in nonprofit management and have a Master's degree in Training and Performance Improvement. I am working towards leaving my full-time career in nonprofit management to become an entrepreneur. In my sales and makeup career, any time I was measured against the goal, I always exceeded it. In youth ministry, I competed against myself to make our services the very best they have ever been. In my current career, I'm the influencer over my team that consistently produce staff members who exceed expectations that the company sets forth.

As an influencer, I share my strength and my struggles with my team and others around me to show that God can still use people mightily even when you don't feel like it's possible. I struggle with dyslexia and anxiety, and the resulting depression from this struggle makes the work that I wanted too difficult but worth it. I know that God uses my influence, honesty and vulnerability to help people live their best for Him.

You are called to be 'the salt and light' in this world. How do you see yourself fulfilling that command by working in the marketplace?

I did research about what ancient people used salt for. In the ancient world, salt was used to pay people's wages. I believe that when God said you are salt, He was saying you are currency in the marketplace. In our day, the term salt is quite common but the meaning is lost. I believe God is saying you are so valuable that you are irreplaceable in the marketplace—you have no substitute for your worth. I've taken this word and applied it to my life and know even when I don't feel valuable that my value is immeasurable.

I also love the fact that the Word says we are the light. Light is designed to eliminate darkness, bring clarity, and end confusion. As believers, we are designed to show the way to people and eliminate confusion. Women of faith are needed in the marketplace to show light and love to people so that they can accomplish their dreams and see the presence of God in their lives.

How do you structure your time to reflect all the priorities and opportunities God has given you to be a light for Him without losing yourself in the process, both personally and professionally?

I had issues with time management in the past. I would try to be there for everyone, and that made me aim for unrealistic standards of perfection. I recently read a book that was a God-sent in this area, entitled *Grace not Perfection* by Emily Ley. This book set me free and has helped me become more patient and kind with myself. It also taught me not to seek perfection but to walk in the grace that God has called me into. I am learning how to properly align my life with God and I allow God to speak to me. Whenever I find myself going to that place of anxiety and tension, I calm down to hear His voice. I find the best time for me to hear God's voice is between 4 am and 6 am. When I reach out to God in the early morning hours, I always hear clearly from Him. When I realize, He is always with me, I find myself living and walking in a place or realm of confidence and rest.

As a woman of faith, how do you integrate biblical and spiritual principles into your work environment with grace and truth?

When I started to really understand that God is always with me, it was so much easier to integrate biblical principles in my work. Good business principles are based in the Bible; treating people with kindness, respecting authority, understanding fairness, and being tough when necessary are all principles based in the word. As a woman of faith, I would add that it's not always easy to live by these principles. I had a situation recently where someone lied on me and blasted me in front of hundreds of people on Facebook. I wanted to respond because what she said was untrue and harsh, but I first took a minute to think about it. I asked myself if this was going to help or cause more drama. I decided not to say anything. I knew saying something was going to cause more chaos than what it was worth. I just concluded that the person could say what they wanted because I cannot be in control of anyone else's actions or comments. With that, I showed maturity by way of tolerance and forgiveness. In the marketplace, you will always meet people with different backgrounds and temperaments, be ready to accept them for who they are.

Everyone needs a "Sabbath Rest." Even God rested after the six days of creation. How do you create space to recharge, refresh, and refocus?

In the past, I never took time off work and I would go until I couldn't go anymore. A few years ago, I got sick and my perspective of rest completely changed. I developed PCOS (polycystic ovarian syndrome), and it has caused issues with my period. There was one incident where I lost so much blood that I became anemic, and the anemia went unchecked because I was so busy working. My blood levels got so low that I was told by the doctor if I hadn't come into the hospital that day, I would've had a heart attack. I had run myself into exhaustion to where there was almost no blood in my body. This was a scary and important wake-up call because it forced me to look at my habits and stop treating my life as if it did not matter. Instead of going so hard without thinking, I started to schedule rest and play. The hospital visit made me realize that the "hard work" that I was doing was stealing life and it was not worth it. Women of faith should balance work with rest if they want to live long, and with peace.

As a woman of faith, what has been your biggest obstacle or challenge in the workplace, and how did you navigate that successfully?

As a woman of faith, my biggest obstacle in the workplace has been balance. In the last few years, my biggest obstacle in the workplace has been seeking balance between time with my family and work. In 2015, my father became very sick and I had to spend a lot of time out of town at my parent's home. I often felt very frustrated and angry that I couldn't somehow do it all. There were times when I was at the hospital with my dad and all I would eat was peanut butter crackers and coffee. When I would come home after being at the hospital for days or weeks, my house would look like a tornado hit it. I couldn't even return phone calls from friends that were checking on me.

At the time, the very best I could do was barely function. There were times I felt very distant from God; even though I prayed every day. I felt like if God really loved me, He would just answer my prayer and heal my father. I was angry at God because I didn't understand how an almighty and powerful God could just leave me in a moment like that when I needed His help. The only way I survived that time was understanding God was with me, even when I was mad at Him, He still loved me.

He used so many people to show His love for me, and I could not deny it. These demonstrations showed me how much I meant to Him. One example of His love towards my family and myself was at my father's funeral. My father's funeral service was held out of town three hours away from my parent's home. We ordered a special uniform for him to be buried in because he was a member of the

U.S. Navy. There was a mix-up that led to late delivery of the uniform and we were under a strict timeline to get this item for the service. The director of the church contacted the driver of the courier truck and chased it down to get the uniform just in time for the funeral home to dress him for the service. At this dark hour, this demonstration of love showed me that God was with me, and He would help me overcome any obstacle.

Have you ever felt 'guilty' for having a career or working? How did you resolve that, and where do you find mentors or support for your journey?

I come from a big family and I always had dreams of having a big family of my own. At this point, I found myself in my late 30s , single and that the dream hasn't happened yet. The option of feeling guilty about having career was never a choice that I've considered. I have always wanted a career as much as I wanted a family. As a child, I dreamed of working, as I saw work as the opportunity to do something that you loved. I've also had the privilege of having great mentors in my life.

Last year, I sought out my current mentor and she has a similar lifestyle as I do. She's a career executive without children and the guilt that I felt about working has always been related to not having kids. I love kids and so for me not to have them at this point in my life is difficult. Seeing my mentor be a great support to her family is inspiring. She raised one of her nephews for about five years of his life when her sister was sick with cancer. This made a huge impact on my life, and I saw that I could still have a great influence without having children of my own. This gave me a sense of freedom that I was on the right path for my life. I understood I could have a meaningful, happy life without having all the things that people say you're supposed to have to be happy.

How did you choose your career, or did it choose you?

My career in public speaking chose me. As I said earlier, I was a very shy and nerdy girl. Growing up, I preferred time in books and with my imagination instead of time with people. I've always loved (I was saved at the age of four years old) God and attending church was my favorite thing. When I was in the seventh grade, I went to my very first church conference. At that conference, there was a youth speaker and he was amazing. In that moment, in my imagination, I saw myself on the stage. I was too shy to even speak up in class but deep down inside, I knew I was supposed to be a public speaker.

Later when I was in high school, I wouldn't even try to use my voice, yet I would be chosen to do projects that required me to act or speak in public. I remember in high school when we had to memorize a poem and recite it in front of class. I recited my poem and got a standing ovation and I did not understand why. I thought that I was just like everybody else but when I spoke, power was released.

If you could give your 'younger self' any advice on integrating your faith life and your work life, what would it be? Would you do anything differently?

If I could give advice to my younger self, I would use one word— relax! In the past, I was so obsessed with trying to figure everything out on my own. I only needed God when I got stuck. I was the classic perfectionist. If I could not do it perfectly, I would not even try. As a younger woman, I also considered failure a deadly sin. If I made a mistake, I would never ask for help. I would just hide the mistake and if possible, I would hide myself to avoid failure. I wish I had allowed more mistakes so I could learn that they are not a big deal but the means to improve on myself.

The biggest mistake is not asking for help when you need it. Making mistakes is really a part of learning and growing, especially for the younger generation. I'm confident if I could go back just 10 years, I would tell myself to not be afraid to travel, and to travel alone if necessary. I know now there's nothing like traveling to open your mind and to give you a sense of accomplishment that is second to none. I would tell my younger self not to compare myself or journey with anyone's experience. I spent the first part of my career working retail at Macy's and I did not like it. I used to say to myself I did not go to college to work in the mall. In those moments, I needed to learn discipline and how to manage my life with limited resources. Working at the mall also taught me how to interact with people and give great customer service. I learned how to connect with people from all walks of life. I needed those lessons because they go hand in hand with entrepreneurship. In those days, I felt like it was a waste of time working in the mall but God was preparing me for my next move.

How has your work challenged your faith, character, or values, and how have you been able to resolve that without compromising?

This past year has been extremely challenging for my faith and my values. In the last 18 months, I finished my Master's degree, and I was promoted in my current job to lead a bigger team, while my father was in and out of the hospital. The pulls on my time and commitments were nearly impossible. There were so many days where I just wanted to give my life to someone else and let them live it. To be honest, I didn't always handle this pressure well. There were many times I would literally disappear from my life because I was so overwhelmed. I also failed one of my classes in graduate school. Although this last year has been one of the most challenging years of my life, God would give me direction when I was at my lowest points.

To hide my pain, I covered my schedule with lots of appointments and busyness, and I took on new projects and things I did not have time for. I would hear God say to me, "Stop and breathe. Take care of yourself." I would have to disappoint many people to take care of myself first. I also had to learn how to count the cost of every decision and not just overly commit and underproduce. I stopped being there for everyone so I could be there for myself. I let go of the shame of not being overly busy and helping everyone so I could help myself. I started to attend therapy and address the root cause of my pain. This helped build my faith so that I could believe God to do the work that He's put inside of me.

Some women feel 'less spiritual' when working in a fulltime career. How do you develop your spiritual life amid a demanding work life?

I strongly believe that God sees me as a leader in my life and family and as a leader, it's my responsibility to fulfill the calling He has placed on my life. For me, that means work. I've learned specifically over the past six months that I cannot walk by faith without asking for and seeking out help when I need it. Making time to develop my spiritual life amid working and taking care of my other obligations means that I must choose to spend time with God purposefully. I allow God to be a part of the smallest parts of my life, for example, in my commute to work, I purposely spend time meditating on the Word. I've found that I get more out of five purposeful minutes of prayer than an hour of pretending I'm connecting to God.

In my faith walk, I've also learned how to rest and not overthink my connection with God. Knowing that He is with me all the time has changed how I approach life, as I have discovered a striking fact — I don't have to figure out anything on my own or work God into my life because He's already there.

What is your favorite scripture, and how has that influenced your role as a woman who works and walks by faith?

My favorite verse of scripture is that Zephaniah 3:17, which says, *"The Lord my God is with me; He is a powerful One who wins every battle. He is a mighty Savior, He takes great delight in me and He calms all of my fears and rejoices over me with loud singing."* This verse is beautiful to me because it reminds me of how God intensely and deliberately loves me. In His love, He is proud of me so I have no fear or feeling of rejection. He rejoices over me with singing. I can walk by faith knowing God is pleased with me. That is all I need!

Zephaniah 3:17, New Life Version (NLV)
The Lord your God is with you, a Powerful One Who wins the battle. He will have much joy over you. With His love, He will give you new life. He will have joy over you with loud singing.

Zephaniah 3:17, New Living Translation (NLT)
For the Lord your God is living among you.
   He is a mighty savior.
He will take delight in you with gladness.
   With his love, he will calm all your fears.[a]
   He will rejoice over you with joyful songs."

Footnotes:

a   3:17 Or He will be silent in his love. Greek and Syriac versions read He will renew you with his love

Learn more about Danita Scott

 Danita Scott is on a mission to empower women and girls to live their best lives. Her professional speaking career is dedicated to helping women identify and interrupt patterns of perfection and failure that hold them back from achieving their dreams. She is funny, relatable and honest about her successes and failures. Danita has a unique ability to connect to people from diverse backgrounds. She has spent her professional career in non-profit management and leading teams to accomplish big goals. Her educational background includes a Bachelors in Organizational Management from Ashford University and a Masters in Training and Performance Improvement from Capella University. When Danita is not helping women live there best lives you can find her chasing after her diva dog Parker, going to the newest thrift store giddy with excitement or traveling to a new city just for fun!

BETSY LAVIN

Tell us about who you are, your profession, and how you use the unique gifts God gave you to impact your circle of influence for His Purposes in the workplace.

Dr. Betsy Lavin. I am a chiropractor and Christian life coach. I live in a unique situation where I have two careers going side by side. Literally. I own and operate a wellness center where half of the building is my chiropractic clinic and the other half is my Life Purpose Retreat and Coaching Center. I call it the WHOLE life approach. It is a nice balance of mind, body and spiritual health. As a chiropractor, I work with physical well-being; as a life coach, I help develop spiritual and emotional well-being.

I love this question about using our God given gifts to impact the world because helping others discover their strengths and giftedness is exactly what I do in my life coaching business. We have all been given great gifts but don't always know exactly what they are with clarity and confidence. Gaining that understanding was transformational in my life.

If you had asked me about my specific gifts in my first few years of chiropractic practice I would have said I'm a good boss and caring doctor. I'm assertive and thrive on change and challenges. Basically, I did what came natural to me. However, I had my life plan done as part of my training to become a Christian coach and my understanding of God's gifts took on a whole new meaning. It changed my perspective on myself as well as those I work and live with.

I learned exactly what my gifts, passions, my values and my strengths were and how God had a plan for me to use all of them. Now I could not only name my gifts, I could claim them as God's divine design for my life. It revealed how God has specifically equipped me for his plan. For the first time, I understood how I am created to be his masterpiece, called and equipped to serve. I no longer had to be everything to everybody, I could just be myself and not feel guilty for saying no to things that were not in my giftedness.

It affected my life so dramatically that I created my own life plan for my coaching business, and currently train other life coaches in their life plan process as well. I discovered that my primary spiritual gift is encourager (exhortation) meaning I walk alongside others to build them up and help bring them to wholeness. This is a valuable gift to have as I work with my team, patients and clients. God has also gifted me with leadership and administration strengths, all essential as a self-employed entrepreneur. Additionally, I have the gift of hospitality which is why the concept of a retreat center spoke so clearly to my heart.

At first glance, it might be hard to connect what my two careers, my callings would have in common, but in revealing my gifts it shows how they all fit perfectly together to glorify God, the creator and giver of my gifts. My purpose driven mentality combined with knowing what my gifts are and who gave them to me allows me to bring God's purpose into every conversation, and relationship I have. When I am in my workplace there are times I can talk openly about my faith and other times where I must keep it personal. However, even in the personal moments I know God is working in me and through me. Just because I can't talk about it, doesn't mean I can't feel it. I pray over my patients all the time, most of the time they don't know it but that doesn't diminish its power.

You are called to be 'the salt and light' in this world. How do you see yourself fulfilling that command by working in the marketplace?

When I first opened my chiropractic practice in rural Minnesota in 1992, I was the only female chiropractor in my area. Add to that, there weren't many women business owners either. I would love to think that I was a perfect role-model for women entrepreneurs seeking to start a business of their own and that I proved to be a good example of how anyone can run a thriving business.

I feel that my personal story of overcoming obstacles is my true salt and light story. You see, I opened my practice in my hometown. People knew me as child, they knew my history of teenage pregnancy and the foolish choices I had made in my young adulthood. To then accept me as a doctor back in their community would take some convincing to show that I had grew up and changed into a responsible physician. I had no idea how well I would be received or if they could put their trust in me. I had to step out in total faith. Thankfully, I did experience my patient's willingness to look beyond my past and received tremendous support. My light of my past didn't diminish the future. Instead I became an overcomer, and an influential survivor. If a teenage mother could become a doctor, there's hope for anyone to achieve their dream career.

How do you structure your time to reflect all the priorities and opportunities God has given you to be a light for him without losing yourself in the process, both personally and professionally?

This area is the greatest challenge for me. I admit I am a purpose driven overachiever and it's a lot more fun completing a task in service to God than it is exercising for an hour. Structuring my time is not the problem, structuring my mindset is. Setting up a daily schedule is easy, making myself on priority on that schedule is difficult.

I find myself justifying my lack of personal care for the sake of doing God's work. When I am doing a large event or project I get so focused on its success that I put my own health last on the list of priorities. Physically I don't exercise because I'm too busy serving my patients and my clients. Emotionally I carry the weight of 'shame-on-me' because I'm supposed to know better. I am a doctor and wellness expert, I know what I should be doing, but fail to do it. Before I know it, my weight is up and my body aches from lack of proper activity. Plus, I'm emotionally weary from carrying the weight of all the "shoulds' I should be doing. I should exercise more, I should stretch more, I should eat only healthy foods. It's then that I turn back to my guiding verse to get me back on track. **I am his masterpiece.** It's me that's valuable beyond measure, not the good works that I do. I honor him when I honor my body, mind and spirit. My "shoulds" turn into I am's. I am beautiful, I am loved, I am forgiven.

While I'd like to say that I have learned the art of setting perfect boundaries, exercising just the right amount every day and eating only the chosen healthy foods, the reality is I am not capable of perfection, only Jesus was. So instead I have come up with a PEACE plan for my personal well-being. I approach my self-care not a process of perfection, but rather a perspective of peace. I make a list of 5 things can I do today that will bring me peace physically, mentally and spiritually. At this moment, my PEACE plan consists of these top 5 things: 1) Drink more water 2) Move my body more (including stretching), 3) Eat at least 3 vegetables each day and cut back on sugar 4) Pray deeper 5) Relax and don't rush God. If I do these 5 things during my day, I will be at peace at the end of it.

As a woman of faith, how do you integrate biblical and spiritual principles into your work environment with grace and truth?

I am fortunate that both of my careers are grounded in faith principles and each allow me to live and talk about my Christian beliefs. As a doctor of chiropractic, a foundational belief is that we are all created to live and heal from the above-down, inside-out, meaning all life is created and sustained from God above, down through us from our inside out. I hold this truth in me with every patient I treat, that God is the source for all the healing.

The patients may not always know this truth, but many do and as their physician it is my job to give God the glory for that healing when I can. I came up with a phrase early on in my practice whenever a patient would comment on how wonderful I had made them feel after their adjustment. I simply say, "I do the work, God does the healing." We all must do our work, so God can do his part. I cherish that in the 25 years of building my chiropractic practice I created a faith- filled environment from scripture on the artwork on the walls to the caring staff who express God's love through kindness and compassion.

As a Christian life coach, every decision that's made is integrated with God's truth and his plan. But it's not always so easy. One would think that running an 'official' Christian business would make sharing my faith with grace and truth easy; when it often makes me question who I am on a spiritual level. It's called imposter syndrome. When called to coach or teach someone, it's easy to fill my mind with doubt, asking who am I to be talking of spiritual matters? "Who am I to be guiding others in their faith walk? You're an imposter; you're not a spiritual expert." Of course, this is Satan's way of deterring me. Instead I look to my verse from Ephesians. I am God's Masterpiece, created in Christ Jesus to do good works, that he has prepared in advance for me to do. Did you get that last part? That he has prepared in advance for me to do. God has fully equipped me for his plan. I am not an imposter, I am a fully gifted, trained and educated life coach. He has prepared you for the work he is calling you to do. Don't ever doubt that the gifts you have are real. What you do matters.

Everyone needs a "Sabbath Rest". Even God rested after the six days of creation. How do you create space to recharge, refresh, and refocus?

On a wall of my retreat center I placed these words as a mantra for my guests: Relax your body, Renew your Mind and Refresh Your Spirit. I use it to share how vital it is to treat ourselves with *retreat* time and allow a place for healing. Retreat times allow us to catch our breath and organize our thoughts, to relax the tension in our bodies and to reconnect with our spirit. They can be super short, one minute mental breaks to full on destination retreats. However, with today's schedules renewal time just doesn't happen, we need to do it with intention and priority.

Maintaining two businesses doesn't allow a lot of time for recharging, but I do make a conscious effort to schedule a few retreats into my everyday routine. If I am working in my chiropractic clinic I schedule 30 minutes of rest time every day. (Rest time sounds more professional than 'nap' time, doesn't it?) I also allow myself quiet time before bed to unwind my thoughts. I struggle most with shutting down my brain, especially when I am working on new coaching project or speaking engagement. I have found the best way for me to disengage my mind is by reading a good mystery novel, something that is not about personal development or finding your life purpose.

When I need a greater divergence, I love to do interior design. I know it sounds crazy because wouldn't that mean more work and more things on my schedule? Yes, that's true, but when I can redesign a new space or redecorate a wall, I feel totally rejuvenated. Since I've redone every room in my house, at my retreat center and my chiropractic clinic; I have resorted to redecorating my friend's homes and business' as my favorite refresher. It allows my creative side to take over and recharges my soul. Ultimately, travel is my favorite time for renew and refocus. A true retreat with all the essentials of beach time, long walks and great companionship with my husband Pete fills me up, mind body and soul.

As a woman of faith, what has been your biggest obstacle or challenge in the workplace, and how did you navigate that successfully?

My biggest challenges are the never-ending changes and setbacks that running two businesses bring. When I created my retreat and coaching business 8 years ago, I had every intention of transitioning out of my chiropractic practice into coaching and speaking full time. However, every time I would gain a little momentum in the coaching business, something would require my full attention back in the chiropractic office. Each time I lay out my plan and step out in faith to activate it, I have a setback. The constant changes in my chiropractic business mean repeated setbacks in my coaching business.

As an example, last week my long-time associate doctor gave her notice that she is leaving the chiropractic profession to raise her family. With that one simple statement, all the hours of strategic planning for my speaking, retreats and coaching business are put on hold while I search for and train a new partner in the chiropractic clinic. Emotionally it's a tremendous shock and it has left me with doubts that I should even bother with the coaching part. It forces me to look at what I am truly passionate about, what brings me the most joy.

That's where faith steps in. I have witnessed God's hand behind the scenes so many times that I have full trust in his long-term plan for me. Do I love this huge transition just when things were starting to going well? Certainly not. But I do love that God sees the whole plan for me and I trust he will reveal it to me in time.

I also ask for help and support with the tough stuff. Running a successful business, whether brick and mortar or online, takes a lot of resilience and perseverance. I simply can't fall apart with every little setback. However, I must be willing to be vulnerable too, to say to my staff, "I can't do this alone. I need your help." Engaging everyone in my workplace with transparency of what is happening builds deeper trust and stronger relationships. Yes, I am the boss and any final decision has to be mine, but to navigate the challenges with grace, I rely on my team for support.

Have you ever felt 'guilty' for having a career or working? How did you resolve that, and where do you find mentors or support for your journey?

Several years ago, I made the decision to down-size my personal chiropractic hours to 2 days a week and start my coaching business from home. My patients would say, "Must be nice to just work 2 days a week." Never mind that I was spending 60 hours working from home building my retreat and coaching business. They made me feel guilty for *not working* full time in the clinic.

The reality is, I had no choice but to cut back. The physical toll has affected my hands and shoulders and I can no longer physically carry a full patient load. At first I defended myself, explaining that I had another job as a life coach and that I worked seven days a week; I had to prove that I was wasn't a slacker. Eventually I saw that it was my pride that was speaking out and I had to surrender it all to God. I gave up trying justify my life choices to others and turned my focus to working for God instead.

I surrounded myself with other like-minded highly driven entrepreneurs who supported me and believed in me. I joined Facebook groups like International Christian Mompreneur Network and iBloom who mentored and encouraged me in both business and personal development. I connected with others who understand the challenges and feelings of isolation that working from home can bring.

How did you choose your career, or did it choose you?

At age 26 I found myself at rock bottom. I was recently divorced, I'd lost my home and now a single mom of a 10-year-old boy. I was exhausted from trying jobs of waitressing and selling Kirby vacuums (for real). I had a big dream of becoming a chiropractor but the obstacles were overwhelming. I was deep in debt with no place to go, except home. A modern day prodigal daughter I returned home to live with my parents while I went to college for 6 years. I had known the power of chiropractic early on in my life and had a passion for natural healing. Earning my doctor of chiropractic degree was the hardest and bravest thing I have ever done. But God had placed a courage in me to walk in faith that I was capable and called to complete it, despite the odds.

Becoming a Christian life coach was totally God's plan at work from day one. Even though I knew the importance of the mind body and spirit in our lives, I never felt qualified for spiritual work. That was for pastors and ministry leaders. I was only trained in "body' healing. God had other plans for me.

About 15 years into my practice, I found myself in a place of being overwhelmed with care giving for my parents. Along with raising a family and running chiropractic practice I soon felt I was so busy caring for everyone else that I had lost myself and lost my personal connection to God. I longed to carve out a day just for me, a day I could dedicate to reconnecting with my faith and have some time to be still.

I thought if I'm overwhelmed with care giving others must be too. I created a Spiritual and Spa retreat and opened my home to five overwhelmed care givers. My gifts of encouragement and hospitality kicked in and soon I was doing several retreats a year with the help of some close friends. I soon learned that if I were to keep this up I would need training, which led me to life coach training. One day after a particularly powerful retreat, I was walking along my little country road, asking God what I was to do next. I felt compelled to do more, to take this retreat concept to a greater level but wasn't sure what that meant. God spoke into my heart that he wanted me to open a full-fledged retreat center. With one huge step of faith and many small steps of obedience, I created my Life Purpose Retreat and Coaching Center. I took training as a life plan facilitator and created my signature life plan, "Find Your Beautiful, Discovering God's Divine Design and Purpose for Your Life."

If you could give your 'younger self' any advice on integrating your faith life and your work life, what would it be? Would you do anything differently?

I would tell her to discover her unique spiritual gifts and God-given strengths early on so she could claim them as her divine design and identity in Christ. I'd love for her to cherish these gifts as her authentic self and live in confidence that she is God's masterpiece. Her gifts are there for a purpose, to build each other up and bring God the glory when she uses them. I'd tell her. "Don't rush God." His plan has perfect timing and that often requires us to be patient as we wait for him to reveal the next step.

How has your work challenged your faith, character, or values, and how have you been able to resolve that without compromising?

I get myself into trouble by dreaming big dreams. I know what I want and I go after it fearlessly. I want success and I want it now. My highly-driven personality tends to push God out of the way as I demand control of my destiny. There's nothing wrong with ambition, but it can be taken too far. I found myself rushing projects and manipulating others to get things done my way. That method doesn't work well with God, as I have come to learn. The many failures I've had in business have come because of my impatience and discontent. For a long time, I was never content because someone else is out there doing it better than me. I had to be the first and the best at everything. That way of thinking is exhausting and frustrating. That's when God taught me all about the importance of patience. He challenges me daily to develop his character traits of humility, peace, and contentment and to walk beside him with my plans and not run in front of him.

Some women feel 'less spiritual' when working in a full-time career. How do you develop your spiritual life amid a demanding work life?

I confess that my spiritual disciplines are not perfect but I'm working on them. I don't always sit down and pray diligently every morning, I don't read and study devotionals consistently. But I do involve God in my life every day. It may not be in a super structured way, but he is at the forefront on all my thoughts. I invite him in through music on the way to work, through conversation and actions with others and certainly in the healing of my patients.

As a business owner I find it helpful to develop my spiritual life by connecting with like-minded Christian entrepreneurs. We get each other, we understand the impact we are making and how vital it is to prioritize faith, family and then business.

What is your favorite scripture, and how has that influenced your role as a woman who works and walks by faith?

My guiding verse is Ephesians 2:10 (emphasis is mine)

For we are his workmanship (his masterpiece), created in Christ Jesus to do good works, (to serve others); which God prepared beforehand, that we should walk in them.

I love to break my verse down as sort of an action plan for my life.

I am his masterpiece.... I am one of a kind with a one of a kind purpose here on earth. No one from the beginning of time to the end of time will be like me. That means I must be significant and serve a special purpose.

Created in Christ Jesus...my identity is in Jesus. I am a child of God, created in his image with all his character traits and strengths in me.

To do good works...I am called to use my gifts to build up others, to serve others in ways that honor God.

Which God prepared beforehand... He has equipped me with all that I need, and has a fabulous plan for me.

That we should walk in them...He calls me to action, to walk by faith not by sight.

Our ultimate purpose is to give God the glory in all we do, to serve others with a heart of grace, even in the secular world. Especially in the secular world. When we work with faith in our hearts, His light is bound to show through.

Learn more about Betsy Lavin

 Led by a strong sense of purpose and calling for her own life, author and inspirational speaker Dr. Betsy Lavin is passionate about helping women discover their giftedness. Her signature coaching program, *God's Masterpiece, Unveiling Your Spiritual Gifts to Reveal Your True Potential helps you* embrace your God-given strengths and giftedness so you can live with focus and clarity of God's call for your life.

She also trains ministry leaders and coaches in her life plan program "Find Your Beautiful" ®, Discovering God's Divine Design and Purpose for Your Life". She is a Doctor of Chiropractic, Certified Christian Life Coach and Certified Personality Trainer.

You can see more of what Dr. Betsy offers at her website: www.betsylavin.com Follow Dr. Betsy on her Facebook page Life Purpose Retreat and Coaching Center

About the Compiler:
Kristi Lynn Olson
Founder and CEO of Women Infused™

Kristi Lynn Olson, Founder & CEO of Women Infused™ Consulting and Media Company, is a consultant, mentor and speaker who teaches Christian women in business how to discover their true calling and define the power of their bigger "Why" as they strategically become women of influence and impact in the marketplace.

She is a woman infused with *purpose* and *spirit*, passionate about helping other high-achieving women define the core of who they are through the lens of their values, gifts, skills, abilities and experience. She empowers women to get a fresh perspective of their unique assignment in the world, develop a personal brand message and create a strategic master plan of action for them to carry out their calling and make a difference in the world.

Kristi hosts a weekly Podcast Radio show called Women Infused™ Radio: Women Business, and Fascinating Faith. She recently launched Women Infused™ Media, a Global Media Broadcast Network that focuses on bringing faith-based personal development and business success principles to women around the world. Her goal is to reach 1 Million Women around the world through her FREE Women Infused™ app. Download the app today, available on iTunes and Google Play.

Contact us at:

Women Infused™ | www.WomenInfused.com

Kristi Lynn Olson | www.KristiLynnOlson.com

Made in the USA
Lexington, KY
15 March 2018